AN ARROGANCE OF IGNORANCE

AN ARROGANCE OF IGNORANCE

One Educator'S Journey from Childhood
Thru the Labyrinth of Life

OSCAR BEAUREGARDI

Library of Congress Control Number: 2021914514

PAPERBACK: 978-1-955955-49-2
EBOOK: 978-1-955955-50-8

Ordering Information:

For orders and inquiries, please contact:
1-888-404-1388
www.goldtouchpress.com
book.orders@goldtouchpress.com

Printed in the United States of America

CONTENTS

This book is dedicated to all of the educators,
academic/nonacademic,
who made the difference in my life.
Their empathy and sage advice made me discover
a fulfilling significance to learning.
Also to Mom and Dad.

PREFACE

After years of prepping for the most important day of school, the first day I came up with a phrase you, the reader will come across numerous times:

"Failure is the condiment for the flavor of success".

I tell any teacher willing to listen that the first day is "imperative" as far as standards impressions made, and in general what the expectations would be.

My "eloquence" to quote, vastly lacking by my own estimates, pale in comparison to most. The reader throughout this book will find many quotes, as appropriate as I deemed necessary and proper. Proper credit has been given to acknowledge those in History who have provided me with empowerment and inspiration, for all the students to understand.

Hoping that after thirteen years of AP World History teaching, the challenges should be greater than the regular class: supplying the above quote should have a more emphatic sense of the direction we were about to head. the right to fail, to try, and try again if necessary, using various techniques and insights offered, should provide the support students would so desperately deserve. Nothing of value comes easy: it comes with struggle-experiencing the "wrong" to get it "right".

"No Student Left Behind" is the credo for most public schools in the state. This is a more than subtle way of sending the message to all who educate our young today. As subtly is their forte....this quote leads to an assumption that all students should be passed! Teachers become less stringent toward the academics: the reason they were hired in the first place! The *personal baggage which I allude to in the read can be infectious for both teacher and student. I estimate that stress is all-consuming and deserves to be addressed, rather than allowing it to become all-consuming: much like the "Leviathan".* **"Buying the Lie" is a familiar saying to the gristled, grunt/teacher: it refers to the pressures peers place or implant upon those who trying to change the status quo in their own way.**

An autonomous teacher appears to be headed to the endangered species list. I lived to tell the tale. Teachers are dropping out like flies: those who refuse the auto tron demands placed upon them by their higher-ups, those who fail to assist students in their most vital needs: to know. Like Diogenes, good teachers shine their lamp to look for a willing student.

There are many opportunities to enhance the experiences of bringing the world into your classroom. I have traveled over the world and brought back many different pictures and artifacts that enhanced the learning process. I continued this after retirement...learning never stops.....

I am a passionate man: this I admitted to as a fault when asked in my interview for the Educational position/job: "What are you shortcomings, as a teacher"? I admitted that I care too much..... This can be a deterrent.

Maybe, if I could take literary license to Emily Dickinson (1830-1886), I can be sum up:

I'm somebody. Who are you?
Are you somebody, too?
Then there's a pair of us-don't tell!
They'd banish us, you know.

Baggage/close-minded/self-important/self-righteous/nay-saying/ oblivious to moral obligation/utilized-brutalized into acceptance and ever popular entitlement expectations:

This is an Arrogance of Ignorance.

A NOTE TO THE READER:

This story is broken into two parts: a Dichotomy if you will. The first part investigates my hereditary upbringing and influences. The second,: how environment plays a role in my and others lives. The learning that one does has a basis in both of these; how much of each is to be determined, in this case, by the reader. Names of characters, places and events are purely fictitious and are changed to protect the guilty from the innocent: the libelous from the true.
Fact Is…. Truth is what you believe……….

PART ONE
HEREDITARY
("I once had a Rocking Horse…he died")
Pop

Growing Up

"What! Another mosquito! I just sprayed insect repellent all over the exposed areas of my skin. Mosquitoes—aka the state bird—are a beast this time of year. It's nice that they went for my face. I must have a face that draws them in.

Just part of a fragmentation of my memory: listening to my father back then, come home to the kitchen table from his job as a printer—a job he realized would soon be outdated—used the words "Face Brute" to describe his boss at the printing press.

Slamming his hand on the kitchen table was a once a week routine.

Ahh yes…the kitchen table—where all good families of the old country meet and greet and "discuss"—and of course, drink.

Growing up, how were any of us, my brother, my sister, or I to know that to "enjoy another drink." "it must be tea time in China," my mother would say and on cue, the Bloody Mary's would pour as if coming from a faucet.

All of us learned to drink from my father would throw out at his chosen, never random, old world slurs. He took great pride in his heritage, but when "Sommina bitch" came out, it was if he had pushed a button on the refrigerator and a can of Schlitz, his beer of choice, came out. We all partook: with brother Chip, the shining star of the family and heir apparent who could do no wrong, helped himself imbibing "slightly" more than my sister or me.

Drinking didn't mean that much to us. Yet, we all learned to drink, eventually.

I guess I could be considered a "Mamma's Boy." Always was and will be. Though Mom's drinking was never given a thought, her heritage implanted a humor with sorrowful existence that I was comfortable with.

Mom could never keep me out of the rain. It was this child's true baptism, to be any one of whatever this fertile mind could conjure: floating homemade boats in the gutter, sliding belly first on the wet front lawn. Most often, Mom would scream at me to "come inside out of the rain!"

"You crazy kid, you're making no sense—come in out of the rain!"

By this time, all the neighbors had seen/heard my shenanigans: running, jumping, playing, even a mock prayer for more rain.

"Ozzie! Get in here now!" Mom would yell.

I would stop; look up at the sky as rain teamed down in immense drops. "Ba- da-deah, Ba-da-dah," I would say, waving in a half-blessing, left-to-right-and back again.

"You crazy kid, I'm going to come out there and get you!" Mom called out. "Come get me! C'mon Mom! If I come in, I may have to take a shower!" Mom shook her head laughing and left me to my improvised, unoccupied, unencumbered life.

Brother and I would both become teachers, he English; I, World History. Mom had doubted my brother because of his "wild days," but she did feel we both would make a good teachers.

Many times I think back to our days to out-do each other. How far and high can we fly off the hill at the bottom of Wilson Street on our bikes: And we FLEW! High and far over the Hump....After a 200 foot start to get up to speed, wrecked bikes were left as mementos of our endeavor. Also, how wide we could turn our sleds when my father dragged us from behind in his Yellow Buick on the barely plowed streets of the neighborhood... Pop enjoyed this as much as we did. We don't worry about "No stinkin' cars"... the weather took care of that.

And the Mosquito man, in his spray truck. One whiff and look out the front... "Mosquito Man!" This call out all kids houses, each kid in the neighborhood mounted their trusty bikes (even if partly bent from the hill) to ride in the fog left by the mosquito truck. "You crazy kids," Mom yelled, "that's poison out there!" "Bah-dah-deeya Bahda-daaah!" and "if it's good enough for the mosquitoes, it's good enough for me," which really makes no sense at all... But we were chasing Kong, and Godzilla: "Confound this fog," and the competition which for our tribal efforts to see who, if anyone could get right up to the truck sprayer itself! One by one, kids got picked off. Some by cars from behind—they got "cut to the curb," off to the side lawn, sometimes by cars in front—curbed on dented/bent front wheels. Today I look back at this and I wonder: the Schwinn bicycle market must have done well. Through the smoke, when you (or whoever) survived "the Mosquito Man" and looked back through the haze. Eerie sounds, some stirring Halloween memories: "clanking" chains, "ouch", and "dammit!" The ornaments in the trees and shrubs was more than a graveyard for bicycles....It was our legacy to flying.

As a first grader, going to Academy School was no fun. Particularly when you already have three strikes against you:

- Living across the Big City River, apart from the area
- Come from parents who were not as "well to do" as other parishioners
- Having a brother who would stand for "no nonsense" and my being perceived younger version.

I was therefore "profiled" at an unmerciful pace. What was I to know? I was in the first grade in a school of God! Adam Sandler, in a movie: He had it right—the nuns were the Penguins; they were the order du jour. The wrong place at the right time—their time. I can remember getting my writing hand "ruler-cracked" by a nun because I did not make my capital "I's" like sailboats. Like my brother, I believed I would sometimes mess up: on purpose. One thing I remember was how unnatural the discipline was for the smallest infraction: feet in the aisle, or whispering. Once, for some infraction too obscure to remember, I was told to "stand and walk up and face the blackboard." Fearing both the nun and the wrath of God, I did what I was told. With a ruler and a wry sneer, she measured my height and dotted the mark on the board with chalk. "You —You, Mister Beau....regardi: You will not move your nose from that dot on the board until I give you permission." And that was it...

To reach the dot, I was to stand on my toes, my back to the class—some (never knew who) threw spit balls at me. "Are you still with us, Mister Beau...regardi?" "Yes, sister," I replied.

When one remains on a blackboard so close, condensation forms from your breath, heavy enough to form liquid. My major concern at that moment was to remain on my toes to keep that dot covered with my nose. 5 minutes, 6 minutes, 7 minutes...

"You wouldn't be squirming, Mister Beau...regardi?" She enjoyed my name too much! "No, sister."

After 10 minutes I was told to sit back down, to the howls and laughter of the class, who were already besmirching my white nose. They had something more to gawk at.

The condensation had turned liquid which gave the appearance of a long drool that went down to the chalk holder at the bottom.

"It appears as if Mister Beau...regardi has a taste for blackboards."

The teacher succeeded in a complete embarrassment of me—to me she was no longer a nun or teacher and would never again be recognized as such: Forget this education. As if this were not sufficient: Something worse was to happen.

This went in part to my request one day to go to the bathroom. The nun refused to recognize me—her excuse later was that she had a class of 40 students and needed to maintain discipline (to the point of kicking our feet out of the spacing between desks aisles - her "posturing" of control). Yep. I peed myself— told myself 'so what: She's that nasty, this way someone would find out. Should have been allowed to go. Shows her anger'. Of course, the student is always wrong, especially by standards of the Holy Order of the Penguins. Again made the fool—by the time my mother had found out, she wouldn't bring it up: she had thought Academy education was best for my brother and I. Yet, I was on an island, alone.

These days as a youngster, it was a psychological torture that made the parochial school—with its rules and school uniforms infamous: a sorted great secrecy of non-sectarian hypocrisy: we were outcast autatrons.

My parents decided their children had "enough." Trying to be like the Jones' didn't work for us, as the abuses escalated.

At the end of my third year there, I was taken by force (hand-dragged— though pulling and yelling every inch of the way) to three different classrooms; forced to wear a girl's beanie cap. "Here's one of our charming young men—I'm sorry, did I say man? Oh, wearing a beanie are you? And, yes, and he wets his pants...I wanted you to know how proud we are of him." Just like the movie, "Carrie" the classes all had a great laugh at me. I pulled away in tears to that echo and found myself outside.

I had finally gotten away, ran from the school after breaking away from the nun. I found myself alone, outside in the parking lot. This was my last day. Walk home? Wait for my ride? Walk? Out of the question! These are stampeding emotions for an 8 yr. old. Their blessed holy demands were met: had I been out into the street and been killed...Then, where would I be? Heaven? Hell? Thoughts a young boy should never have to consider.

"Okay" I repeated out loud—public humiliation in a private school. And this is what God, the God I learned from this school, intended for me—or for that matter, anyone? What would Jesus do? How about what would He say!? Consider it a lesson learned. We would be off to public school the following year.

But when I "went off" about this religious "residue", Mom gave me the Palmolive soap—no Ivory for me! I didn't like it, but I also didn't feel it was fair. So I ate half of it and tried like Alfalfa in "The Little Rascals": to blow bubbles. I'd blow a few into the air, and we both laughed.

Yet, the belt was always waiting for Brother Chip and I, had we gotten into any of our many blowouts. Working on the Hut was sibling therapy. The hut that we built in the backyard forest was the talk of the neighborhood. It was two stories high, set on 4-by-4 plywood from nearby buildings going up. *They'll never miss it,* we thought. Roof tile topped it off. You want to join The Hut Club? Sleep out and we would sleep upstairs and lock both the outside and the upstairs trap doors where four could sleep comfortably. It would be at about 1a.m. that the fun began. We would drop on the bottom floor out from where the "newbies" were bunking, a pack of firecrackers!

Popping, cracking, yelling "Look out! Get me out of here!" We just had to watch the madness that ensued. Once the newbies were on the move, we'd break the lock and watch them run out the door. What the neighbors thought: their must have transpired a subtle understanding: "Those Beauregardi boys."

Then there was Hugo "The Hammer" Hammershall. With his weight at over 200 lbs by the age of 10, to us he was "Hammer" We rode our bicycles behind the mosquito fog machine during the summer. Boys need something to do other than obsess over who was the toughest kid on the block.

Hammer and I invented a game with our bikes: "Sir Lancelot and the Dark Knight." It was Hammer versus me. He could kick me off my bike in one smidgen of a touch of his mano a mano, pointed six-foot spear against my chopped off long stick. At

100 ft apart, we came at each other. Hammer was slower than I: But I had a plan.

He picked up speed as I was also slow to start. He aimed for my chest, but at full speed and the point of attack, I stuck my lance into his spokes. I saw Hammer stop dead to a flip in the air—a complete Hammer-toss 360 degree flip! Then he landed on his head!

Anyone else would have needed an ambulance, but not "The Hammer". "I think I have to go home now," he said as he picked up what remained of his broken Schwinn and left. I noticed that where my foe had fallen. The Hammer had left a two-to-three inch dent in the paved road…. with his head! From then on, it was known as "Hammer's hole."

Brother Chip wanted in on the medieval action. He picked up a garbage can lid and part of my broken stick to duel with me. I ran into the woods and found the largest branch making sure I could swing it. We dueled in the midday sun on Apache Avenue with two garbage can lids, his spear and strength, and my club and determination. Joey struck a few times.

"Hah! Hah!" he yelled with every successful jab.

I had bided my time. I bashed in his garbage lid. "You're gonna get in trouble," he said.

That didn't stop me, especially when the neighbors watching and listening to the loud "Clang! Back! Ouch" sounds coming from the front street. It wasn't their garbage lids. Mom watched too, from the front door.

Anyway, I was the first in the neighborhood to back my brother off in front of all the other kids.

"Get in here right now!" Mom yelled.

My brother backed off and into the house he went. I held that club high in the air. "Odin!" I yelled and may chivalry never die.

My father had the oddest expression later, when we were eating dinner; with a long-like club branch leaning next to the refrigerator by me, We all knew Dad meant business…… and Dad's business was beyond law.

"Don't ask," Mom said to Pop as we ate. Mama la Sabe toda! I had a sleeping partner that night.

I remember at a very young age when an "air of defiance" became a part of me. It was at Grandpa Gorski's house, a farm and country style home with a large swing fence. He never drove a car as far back as I can recall. He had a full plot of vegetables stretching from the driveway over. He had built the house after his naturalization/certification, and it was one of the few houses with an outhouse, a potato cellar and a farm with a barn, bee hive and rabbit hut and water well, complete with a bucket.

It has been said that his brother, Bushka would sit at the far end of the long, maple, heavily varnished living room table while saying little to anyone (challenged in English, most likely), and would be reading the morning paper. Unbeknownst to only him, he was reading it upside down!

Mom and all of her brothers and sisters, totaling 9, would be laughing so hard. This education was testament to their lives of the old country; located in Eastern Eurasia.

Grandma's first name was not known to me, ergo I knew her only as "Grandma." I've heard that my original grandmother was "put away" by my grandfather for being "unbalanced." Some claim it was all too much for her. Others say she was crazy. No one bothered to wonder who or what happened to her, until the deaths of my 2 Aunts . "They didn't take their medicines," was the reasoning.

Grandpa was stern, but fair. This I shall remember! I loved the days when his friends from Eastern Eurasia would come over and play cards and drink vodka, playing the balalaika. Sometimes, they drank the homemade cherry wine from Grandpa's cherry tree or Dandelion wine. In later days, these natural made drinks made for many "hippies' to REALLY want to try some. The long-haired dissidents were more than happy to imbibe, freebies being "so cool" though I can surely claim I was not a part of that craziness. Grandpa nicknamed me 'Toe' for being capable of picking up dimes from the floor with the nimblest of toes.

One day, I went to the back of the vegetable plantings to the barn where a mule had existed. There was a rabbit hutch there where Grandpa would skin, slice, and dice his dinner. In between was a chicken - fenced in hen house. Plastic Easter eggs were planted in the nestlings of the chickens in the belief that the chickens would be motivated to hatch more eggs. "True-True," said Grandpa.

When I was about 5 yrs old and liked to listen to the hens' small talk. I even fed them the older corn not given to the rabbits. But one time, after watching a few chicken fights in the penned area, I promoted my own Dance and Swwwwing Forum extravaganza. I threw stones at the chickens.

"Squawk!" I heard as they flashed, fluttered and jumped. I had not expected that sight. Then I saw an even more unexpected sight: the rooster of the house saw me, JUMPED the seven foot high chicken wire fence and chased after me, up the dirt driveway.

I thought I ran fast, but the angry rooster ran twice as fast as I. He caught up to me as I fell, jumped onto my head and started pecking. I couldn't get him off. Grandpa and Mom came running over. With one hand, Grandpa took the rooster, grasping its neck with his fist. With one thumb down and one motion, he twisted its neck.

"SNAP," we heard. We watched the rooster run and flutter in a pattern-less death dance. I was still sore, but more ashamed of letting a rooster get the best of me.

"You see? You tea-zing rooster, you get hurt. Eez good for you," Grandpa said with his Thick-as- Borscht accent.

"Yeah, and it's good for you too!" through my tears and frustration.

Laugh? It's unusual, but not so much for his cultural heritage way.

We were invited back to Grandpa's farmhouse for dinner the next day. He served-guess what?

"OzBie. You eat... this bigger plate than everyone else have here.

It makes you strong like bull. Put hair on chest. Eez good for you," he told me.

I ate it all. Thanks for that, and the borscht, Grandpa.

I still have his certificate of naturalization dated 1940. His name upon reaching the United States as an immigrant is Lubabacci Ghorinski. It was ultimately shortened to "Gorski."

The powers existing then regarding the US immigration policy indicated on his certificate the he had immigrated from Poland, not Russia, due to anti- communist sentiment existing then pre-McCarthyism. It was Stalin purges that he was escaping from. The back of the certificate had his name changed from Sobababacci to Bob. I guess that name sounded more American, but it was Grandpa's character that kept the ethnicity alive. He would later laugh at the remarks of Khrushchev—"capitalists" and "we will bury you." All used in my U.S. History class.

Some of his children, when we were much older and married, would ask him about their heritage during the Cuban Missile Crisis.

"Grandpa, teach us to say 'Don't shoot comrade.' We are like you."

He would just laugh and not really give much credence to any of the news....Fear.

How I knew what it could do, even to my own family and to most Americans (still today). They would run to the grocery store to buy batteries, rakes, snow shovels, salt for ice, and milk and bread. It amazes me how much power the weatherman has. Fear is a motivator.

"You don't need a weatherman to know which way the wind blows," Bob Dylan once said. Or was he speaking of the 1960's radicals? It applies either way you think of it.

In my neighborhood, it's not like that anymore. My brother and I would look down the street and about three hardball, two bats and our gloves; we would walk down the street. We'd walk up to the houses and knock on the doors and yell, "EYOKEE!"

We were like Terrance Mahoney and Satch from the Bowery Boys . We started the neighborhood baseball games.

We'd get a good dozen or so number of kids together and play in an open lot that we cut with lawn mowers and made it the infield. It was pure dirt with stone and glass between two unconnected streets. With a backstop of chicken wire and poles hammered in, we'd play all day. Sometimes a ball got lost in the woods. That was an automatic home run. As for sliding, we didn't care about it. The marks we dug into the ground would be permanent and ripped pants would tell who won.

Oz Beauregardi—strong arm, no fielding, weak bat. Hitting a double was a personal triumph.

Once, I joined the Little League team known as the Broadstreet Bulls . It was the worst team to ever play the game with two-year record of one and twenty one. When I was named as one of the All-Stars of the league, (no one else would go) I was not ecstatic, but apprehensive and to be honest - fearful. I dropped a ball with the bases loaded and spiked my own foot because I had to wear Chip's shoes for luck.

Upset, I was laughed at by the other team, and my own team hated me. Later, with two run outs and a runner on, I was at bat. The emotions running over me were palpable. The opposing pitcher was throwing too hard for me to connect the bat. He threw his first fastball <u>at</u> my head! So this is part of the great American pastime.

But our coach was human. He sent the runner to steal the next base and was thrown out there for the third out. Looking back, I can remember all that swelled inside me. It was everything that had made me who I was and was not. Maybe it was an epiphany. I did get to see a pitch thrown at me, like I needed more intimidation from opponents. But I was in that batter's box again.

My father would hit us fly balls after that, and Chip said the Bulls were thinking of cutting me because of my fly ball mishaps. I took away pressure put on me…. and flatly resented it.

One day, Dad made a rare appearance at a game. He saw me drop a fly ball hit right to me. At that point, he walked away from the game, never looking at me. I was not my father's son then. In the next inning, I was hit by a fastball square in the left temple from an out-of-control young opposing pitcher. At that time, batting helmets had no ear flaps. They were plastic baseball caps.

No frills/protection.

I took my cap, small crouch, stood as tall as God would allow…. started walking toward the pitcher's mound, pointing my bat at the pitcher.

"You Somma bitch," I yelled. Then, I collapsed.

I took my base, and then sat out on the bench for the rest of the game.

At sundown, I had no way to get home other than to cross the gully between the neighborhoods surrounded by woods. The gully was a good 150-foot deep ravine caused by the sewerage and excesses of water that came up through the railroad tracks to what was known as "Shirley Lake." (Go fish there, come home saying "Aw S…" But this part of Shoe Lake had no fish, but frogs and mosquitoes. I took the shortest cut I knew home and climbed down the ravine, crossed said stream and started to climb up the ravine.

But the shortest way I had learned was not the easiest. Never is.

The ravine's incline was almost a complete 90 degree angle from the bottom. I grabbed onto vines for support, dangling my bat and glove, and did my best Tarzan interpretation.

It wasn't enough that I was stuck, and the pain in my head quickened. It throbbed in a way I had never experienced except for the immediate impact. I put my bat in my trousers, dropped my glove on one hand and hugged the filth of Sure Shirley Lake for as much time as I can remember. I had passed out against a wall of muck, but wouldn't let go.

The drop was enough to kill a man and I was about 20 feet from the top. By the time I awoke it was pitch black, but the pain had subsided. I went along sideways like a crab to finally reach the top at someone's backyard in my neighborhood. I walked home, not pushing it, but still dizzy from the strain and pain. I got home, showered, and went to bed.

My father came to me later. *My God, I thought. What does he want from me now?*

"Coach called and said you took a pitch to the head. Are you okay?" Dad asked.

Am I okay? Inside I was laughing like one of those Pagliacci clowns. "Yeah, I'm okay," I said.

The pressure to my left temple still exists today. I knew a hospital was out of the question with finances being what they were. No mention of the dropped fly ball at all. My commented thoughts were the last words my father would say to me upon my last visit with him on this earth.

Money was not the extravagance that others had in the neighborhood and my family protected me from this and prejudice. The one thing I took pride in before all this happened was when Dad went to the "Rag Man" in Burnside. "The Rag Man" collected rags for sordid reasons, but would not give my father the $5.00 he had requested for a duffle bag filled with rags. Seeing this, I knew this would be a "piece de resistance" for all time. I took my shirt off, gave it to my father and said, "I don't like this shirt. Let's add this in."

The Rag Man stalled, stared and then gave my father $5.00 as requested. I swelled with pride, but said nothing to my Dad. Mom asking why I was shirtless: I wonder how the Rag Man felt.

THE RAGING BULL OF APACHE AVE.

It was the International Boxing Match of Apache Avenue and Walker Avenue. We had used four-by-four wood, taken again from the buildings along the highway. We cut up old garden hoses and made to strips nailed to the set posts in a square "ring" about 12 feet apart.

The main event showcased the two heavyweights in the neighborhood. It was not Hammer: He was a peaceful giant whose mother would NEVER allow her son to be a part of this brutality.

The newly moved in English Champion who has "traveled across the Atlantic just for this fight: Calvin "The Conqueror" Ganderson."

He was not as big as Hammer, whose own mother refused to watch the fight..

His opponent, seeking redemption for the one onslaught that kids would throw at him for his size of 215lbs was Jimmy Mitchell. I have to give him credit for showing up. The smile he gave off at the sound of hearing his name announced: priceless. The fight was of non-interest: The Main Event was not even fully determined yet!

The whole neighborhood—mothers, sisters, little kids trying to sell gumdrops at double the price, hangers on who would want to be trainers, kids from other neighborhoods—Came out to watch. Sorry, Jimmy: but word travels fast once the ring was constructed.

Guess who was the Main Event card?—Chipper the Destruct o (a cartoon character made of metal with claws) Beauregardi. The braggadocio announcement: "Who wants to fight me? C'mon, anyone dare to accept my challenge? I'll take on anyone."

"This intimidation stops here" I thought. Besides, the deafening silence was a neighborhood embarrassment.

Chip had a good 5" and 25lbs more on me, plus, he was older. "I warn you Toe, I'm not going to take it light on you." A loud and imposing threat: once again establishing primogeniture, not just for family, but for the neighborhood. I had an interesting advantage.

My brother's best friend from school Ernie C.— top student, short, no big sports but was a golf wiz: An all-around nice guy (those two made quite the interesting "odd couple"), was my manager in my corner. This "event", interestingly enough, had the whole neighborhood on my side. Impetus was with me and Ernie was tarp as a shark (an after the fight euphemism). "Keep low, make him punch down, and he will tire after this round; if he throws hay makers and you know he will, sneak in what body blows you can, then, work up…just keep your hands up to protect your head and any knockouts—we both know he wants it, <u>bad</u>, after that booing he just got (the neighborhood didn't care for his bravado upon his intro); he did take a verbal assault, particularly from many mothers there.

No one remembered to bring a bell, so the referee, who I wasn't even focused on, just said "DING!" Another moment of truth versus fact to emerge: Joe tried his "shuffle" and started to use his reach advantage. I became a crouch and stay close defender, covering both sides of my head (still more than a little leery of that fastball in the temple), dipping and swaying in a left-right motion. Chip stopped and unleashed a flurry of hard lefts and rights in rapid succession, no chance for me except to get closer and butt him with my head. Chipper as usual complained and that's when I went after him with the same attack mode I endured. He covered up—a menial victory. Chip came back, realizing the crowd had cheered my flurry. I retaliated with and got "pissed." He kept throwing long hay makers. I kept sneaking beneath head to left head to right and got some body shots in. Two minute round was up. THE CROWD ROARED APPROVAL! I had no idea if I won or lost the first of this three round testament to be…Chip was still "pissed" (no other means to relate what his attitude was at this very moment).

Chip said, "Toe? I'm going to let you know right now, you better quit, you're my brother, but I won't slack off like before, if you come out again. But if you think you're going to beat me, quit now.

I took it easy last round and I really don't want to hurt you." Hurt me?! This was intimidation that was often used like: when mischief night came around and the bags of shit lit on front porches and garbage cans filled with water leaning on top of roofs. This all came back to me then; no faking it, when Chipper hit me, it hurt, but there are all forms of hurt that I was learning at this very moment of my life. If I back down now, who was I then? I'd be my brother's lackey! That's what! And that thought went beyond anything else I could consider.

Ernie said, "Man, you did great, keep your hands up and, bob and weave your head if he loads up on you, I know you feel it. I got you ahead on points. Just keep doing what you did—he's a big bluff anyway." I hope Ernie knows what I don't!

Courage or stupidity? "DING!" Too late to decide now—and the Raging Bull of Apache Avenue came right at me as I fainted left and defended right. Chip was swinging harder now, I could tell from earlier and he was looking for some redemption. I had to get inside to avoid these constant long, heavy blows; I covered up, ducked and started back on his body. He wouldn't drop his hands, he kept throwing, and I wouldn't go down, not for my last breath.

Pummels upon pummels, I could hardly get a punch in, got backed in a corner covered up a shot a few lefts and rights as my brother's arms were wearing down—A BATTLE OF ATTRITION, but I was learning the hard way, about my brother (about persistence).

This wasn't baseball! This was something bigger.

"DING!" People were yelling at Chipper for being a bully. I just lifted my left as if to say "I'm okay." Ernie had ice to put on my face and cool me down. "Can you do it, Toe? One more round? Can you finish what you started? I'm proud to be in your corner—think like this—win the last round—win it and everyone will know—even your brother: respect is earned. Just have to get in more punches than him…Protect the head, duck and weave, but throw as much and as hard as you got. You'll never be sorry you did."

"Toe, I'm not holding back anymore," said Chipper, "I don't care whether you're my brother. I don't want you hating me, but I'm not gonna pussy foot around this time—just end it now. Walk away and quit. I don't want to hurt you!"

There's that word again: Quit. Did Mom and Dad ever quit? I surely did not want my mother's sympathy as she was coming over to my corner—I waved her away. This was _my time,_ my moment, not for glory but to stand up for just being who I was.

I look down at Chip's corner—he was tired, too many punches that mostly hit their mark when my head got in the way. "Look at him Toe," said Ernie, "he's gassed... breath deep as you can right now. Get that air in! Don't let him intimidate you. One to go, give it your all!" Really not much to think about at this time: survive: then try to out punch him. A long rest between rounds...

"DING!" Round three and final round! Again the Raging Bull—this time met by my hard head to his fists, then my head to his belly. I backed him up, he was ropa doping, but the rope-hose was giving way. I saw him move and throw a right cross that hit the same left temple I had always protected. Stumbling... Chip got angry again but now I came after him. I knew at this juncture, I had more to prove. I had more will than he did. Thinking back, the shame of losing to his little brother must have more than crossed his mind.

Pride (comes before the fall) in this case forced my brother back to stick and jab, stick and jab and my return to crouch to get some breath, yet I was finding more body than head shots. Mom in the background: "Stop it you two: Stop it right now! "My response as I backed away: "Badda-Dia, Badda-DA".

"DING!" End of fight. "Honest" kids in the neighborhood had it: 3-0 Chip, 2-1,Chip, 1-1 even. I lost, but I won. I don't very often think of that day, but when I do, I'm not so much in consideration for myself—I look at "Rocky," "Rudy," and "Raging Bull;" some of my moments come back. But I wonder, really wonder: what must have gone through my brother's mind and heart when facing his younger brother (22 months apart) in the squared circle. I had already caught him off guard just by accepting his challenge (I even let the moment sit, to savor my acceptance). During this mauling, where two brothers, in front of all to see, expressed their desire to extend into adulthood and share/show all what follows—had I only considered; just one quick moment in the clinch; I'd pull my chin up over his shoulder and for no one else to hear - but him: whisper, "I love you, Chipster."

And then I'd catch him with a right hook that would roll his eyes into the back sockets and I would give him the "Champion/ stare down" that a knocked out fighter had no choice but endure. A little dance would have been nice too, if I had the strength.

OUTSIDE THE NEIGHBORHOOD

It's an eye opener for me as a very young adolescent. We had already switched to public school—Lakeview. Unbeknownst until my late high school days at Lakeside that the school wanted both my brother and I up one grade. Mom felt different about it. I immediately remembered my father's outrage at my spelling grade: "D" and that outrage followed ("Sommina Bitch, with me working everyday on typesetting-you're gonna improve on this!") would be extended to sitting at the backyard picnic table— spring time and my sister T.C. watching, playing "Scrabble"—my father knew me better than I did myself. He humiliated me at the bowling alley, too—he loved it, the ball too heavy for my "frame." "Look at that girl, in the next lane, how she throws." "Cut it out Pop!" But I was no match for her, taller and skinnier, and about same age as I, and Pop? He just quit after one game. He tried, but I was set on bigger ideas: Football! Yes. It was a passion for my brother, father and very much so, myself...Frank Gifford, Y.A. Tittle, Dick Butkus, Hornung and Taylor, and Jim Brown. These were Gods of that time. Ferocity - tenacity: I had to try.

Minors football, last year of eligibility and I joined—first string offense and defensive lineman (yes I played both ways) and second string running back. Marty Toms, a quiet unassuming yet larger than us guys, was #1 in both running back and linebacker: Minors rules age? I believe 13 by a certain date, but weight?

We were good—very good—Marty Toms would score some 5 touchdowns a game. Berdy Zagorski, the neighborhood athlete down the street, threw like Johnny U. Found the pocket and let it fly 30-40 yards and on the mark (he went on to a state champion win against Parsonville in his senior year of high school, one year after my graduation). But he would say to the huddle—"I got all the time in the world back there. Just wanted to let you guys know." "Hey Birdman," I told him, "pose one time like Johnny U. You may get your picture taken." My father had already talked up his son's accomplishments on the team at work—there should be a press photographer. He got it—a moral victory! And my father, I could hear, as I stood in the mud for a punt on a rain soaked afternoon at Jonesville … I hear from the sidelines my Pop yelling "Rrrrrrooobbie-Doo."

One time my brother snuck out of the stands, while I was halfback, drew up a play to circle me around the coverage on the outside—"And you'd better catch this! By now, Chip knew that we were Tittle to Shofner of the neighborhood. No way to be stopped—circled around, no one there—my only touchdown. And to celebrate? Just letting the ball slide out of my hands. Like it was an everyday occurrence. "Way to go Rroobie Doo" Mom and Dad and my sister Pin (Penelope: who was an honorary cheerleader).

Sidelines party! My only touchdown in Minors but one I savored as did the family—Pizza night! Chipster...... Thanks.......

Next day I was invited to Walt's house—still in Academy school but a great friend. But he wasn't there, but his sister Wanda and the girl two doors down, Dawn, were. Dawn was practicing for a play. I believe it was "Guys and Dolls" and needed a male reader. Both girls had some type of thing towards me. Wanda left for snacks inside and Dawn sat very close to me and said, "You are so cute, I want to kiss you." I said, "Well..." That's all I got in before this "smooooooooooch." What did I know? "Did you like it?" "Yeah I guess it was nice" (not like my Mom's for sure). She gave me a weird smirk and left. Oh well....

My neighborhood paper route (of course my father's Burnside Record [now defunct & sold piece meal to specialized medical teams) allowed me to contact with many girls, but work was my "piece de resistance." I could earn money and not have to depend on hitting my father for cash (side note: I always cut the front and backyard for the old man "en gratis"—just thought it was the right thing a son should do). Across Highway 14 to Norman's, there were no barricades to separate the large traffic to and fro Lakeside and Burnside. It's where we got the needed wood and supplies to build out backwoods, two-story hut. The place to go was to Normans, though, named after its owners. I would stick to the normal: Slim Jim's and a Yoohoo or baseball cards, always the bubblegum inside and those sick Bazooka Joe Jokes: "Knock-knock who's there? Boo! Boo who? Don't cry...it's only me!" AAARGH! Many a summer day was spent arguing about the finesse of the snap and taste that came from the Slim Jim— bordering cultist. We'd follow the mosquito man on summer days through the poison smog; sleep out in the hut. I had to wait for baseball to be over for football. Though I did improve (couldn't get any worse). Arguments over Willie Mays, DiMaggio, and Mantle were always there. Oh yes—Baseball Cards were as great as the players......no trade of DiMaggio for Ted Williams! YES!

At football I had found my niche (though I never found out from Dad what a Roobie-Doobie was). By the time I was a freshman in high school, I had experienced the death of JFK (after getting sweet-talked by a fellow cute classmate for my BB glove to borrow.

The hurt teachers showed that day was felt by all of us. When 9/11 would happen, so many years later, I found myself in that same awkwardness, but this time I saw it or it was happening at that moment, with my students. First thought: accident. Who could be so blatantly angry and hostile to act in this more- than-brutish attack? Then, the truth would show; a second plane crash.

"Oh my God's" were pouring out as students of other classes poured in…"what channel"… "I got family out there"…"Mrs. W. won't let us watch it!" The unknown can be a dangerous, nasty, insidious thing: not knowing what others "claim." This was no accident and my classes saw it with their teacher. I told them almost in a political correct absurdity, "If you know how to pray, or care to, let's give a moment of silence for our own intentions." Religious and public: a great combination.

Kennedy's was radio broadcast and all teaching stopped. When the Zapruder tape was issued: one could see (or choose not to for I have always said choice is freedom) right after the corner billboard, JFK's head pushed forward and Gov. Connolly's head turning to look over his right shoulder. But the second shot and blatant and cruel blow that show parts of JFK's skull shatter and the head violently pushed in a back-sideways motion. Then Jacqueline Kennedy crosses back to the FBI agent to help him aboard as the car sped away. Thought: What would have happened had it rained that day? Could a form of Pope-mobile been issued? At least a top was a thing that could deter the assailant(s). Why is this NOT taught in US II? I pushed and pushed for it every year.

Other political killings ensued—MLK, Bobby Kennedy, etc. Watching the old neighborhood attempt to live through its "Silent Majority" and do their everyday business. Just how does one ignore all this? There was still Vietnam! While teaching, I would never ignore the '60's.

These tumultuous '60's had made of me a more 'driven individual.' Who to believe? Who to trust? Blood would pour out on the TV. Pop who would never talk of WWII and the family he snuck through lines to help…never a word. He once mentioned to me privately "If you do ever go over there to see them be sure to be nice to them."

Autumn as a kid—my brother wanted to have a party downstairs with some girls. Beatles, Rolling Stones made us dance till we dropped. A good time was expected by all. But like Pop would say, "You always find out who a person truly is when they're drunk."

And Chipper was "lit": carried to the cellar by two girls —I snuck away, peeking at the non-"action." The girls danced the guys who also drank. My brother, always perceptive, even in his "state" offered me the rest of his Thunderbird—"What's the word? Thunderbird! What's the price: twice as nice." It was more than half a quart and I started in, coming out, in more than one way.

Then, as my brother was helped by friends to a bathroom upstairs, one girl came up to me, alone, maybe a few years older than me, long dark hair and brown eyes round as tea saucers. "You know I've heard about you. I think you're cute," she said. My mind went racing. Whoa! Older woman and drinking Thunderbird ("The Life of Riley" and I was no William Bendix). She grabbed my face and started to make out with me. It was an "All or Nothing at All" (Frank Sinatra) give what you can and follow her lead. She leaned in and held me closer. Chipper and the rest then came back down and she split off to the other side of the cellar, great for my ego, but to continue would have probably given my brother some competition and an embarrassment for her. Could this be an issue (this 15 sec "interlude")? My brother was defiantly building up a reputation. My parents allowed this because they had an eye on my brother to not allow him to get in an accident—him or anyone else for that matter. They also knew of our drinking expertise (growing up). Rebellious natures were the norm and we were a little too young to play the role of the defiant "social non- conformists."

Arrest and drug addiction were the words that they feared.
Joe and I: "Hey Pop, what did you do in the war?"
Pop: "Nothing; get me a beer!"
And when so much mail arrived from Paris and Pop hardly sending a word (that <u>we</u> knew), it became a subject "no lo contend-re": "not to enter." But he did say, "Neither of my boys will be partaking in this Vietnam. No way would I let you go, you can live in Canada or hide away—but not any of this." There

was no "Somma Bitch" until the Vietnam draft came out. Instead of spending time with my Mom due to her illness, Pop had spent a number of years at the Burnside Record trying to maintain the status quo. He had to, it's all he knew. Money was getting tighter.

In High School, the protests of the 60's raged: Chipper went to Harding and I was pushing my way through the antics/gimmicks of being related to someone "popular". I had always felt that I was more than "Chip's brother"....As I struggled to make my way on an everyday basis, I would get the daily "How could your brother be so cool and you be so lame"? I figured this is where I developed the phrase I would often use in my classrooms : "I guess I have failed to live up to YOUR expectations". They kept up the comparison anyway, and I kept up not caring. There was a greater reality for me: Mom's illness: Their opinions pale in the comparison to what I was dealing with. But I did love football, so guess what?

Varsity football's head coach, Tom T., of the HS, missing his finger, and Chipper got cut from it his junior year. Mr. T went down the line—"Dilly's haircuts Barbershop; tell them Mr. T sent you, it'll be cheaper." The freshman players lined up. Mr. T went down the line picking out who needed it, "You, you, you, you, you—YOU." My hair was not that long, but the coach had a championship team (many who knew Chip). If you cut your hair, it meant you were from the team.

Was my Mom surprised to see the buzz cut I got! The neighborhood gawked at what had transpired. I went to bed and knew this was "heavy," as those Anti- ar hippies would have said.

But hair grows back and football was just starting. So the tears were short lived and Chipper silently understood.

Two-a-day practices would be cut to one because of the overcrowding at school. We would run sprint after sprint after sprint then laps then more sprints. We were all being measured to be cut and gone or make the team. I was one not to quit.

Some puked, some walked off, and some just didn't belong on a field. I had some great Minors training—knew the basics, but was still only 115 lbs. "You smaller boys want weight? Start eating steak, plenty of mashed potatoes, bananas, and Metro cal." What the hell was that? I tried it for a week—went up a total one pound in two weeks.

A lineman?! Couldn't push the "sled," had to find some place, and I would not go down: not for Chip at boxing— not for them, either (Somma Bitch).

Hot August, the days seemed like sweat-and-puke a-thons. One on one exercises: laying on your back, helmet to helmet. The ball placed between the two players. "On the whistle", was the command to prepare mentally and morso physically. My heart was racing to anticipate the sound: "Got to get the jump on that other guy to get the ball". The ball is everything! And, if you get beat at the ball, you'd better get the better of your opponent. Thought how I would move forward first, plotted it and, BLLLP: Shoved my elbow behind my back and turned with a hip reaction to kneeling position. One foot off the knee and the ball was mine! By the time I scooped the ball, juked to the left and went right, free hand to stiff arm or push the stunned opponent. Minor's football and baseball gave me a developed edge.

"Whoa" said the Frosh coach, Ron R. Mr. R, remembered me from a Minors game he refereed. He penalized my team 5 times, me, in a row, for my, let's just call it, "verbiage". Only within his earshot, though. Now, what's he thinking?

After a few more head "banquets", this day was the final day of cuts: the coaches had throwing kids left and right into the showers.

But now it was two on ones…running back with a blocker, and on the other side was the linebacker/tackler. Guess which one I was…..The blocker was about 30 pounds more than me: and I knew his every move. "I can beat this guy" to myself. This is my moment. This is exactly what I've always been: never taken by false bravado…Fear this? With the whole team around us, I again gave the matter thought before the whistle: he's coming right at me: let him….BLLLP; Came up right after his initial charge, elbow the shoulder/neck and shoved him away to tackle the charging ball carrier. Clean and beat him to the contact. "Nice" said the blocker.

"Whoa" coach R.R. was off the wall, now! "Yeah, Yeah... This little SOB has something going". My secret, coach (maybe ours?). "Give me another blocker" same result with a different tactic: using his weight against me, I pushed him back as if he was the sled I couldn't push....with the two duffle bags we were to work between, this would force the running back to hesitate. Finally, when his weight was applied, I shouldered around him and was taken backward to make the tackle.

The running back had a reputation in school as a tough, Bad Boy.

Rumors spread [as they most often do in school] that this guy worked the night shift at the graveyard [I like to believe he was likely to have started that rumor]. As I was getting up, the team had been for tough AJ, but the crowd was now turning for the underdog: the one supposed to get cut: Hey Pop: shirt off my back, Pop. And R.R.? He was pacing and out loud shouting: declaring his disbelief, he also gave AJ a few jabs, verbally. "Give me two blockers, I want two!" Two newer guys, expected to make the team, blocking for AJ. This is all on me...if I want to play so bad, I'll just have to play this fast and hard: in that order. "BLLLP" and the moment that I realized, even at this young age, was to be.

One blocker hit low, as I stumbled forward, the other high. "Don't go down now." High hit allowed me to step over the first blocker to confront the charging gravedigger. The blockers are now behind me, no footing. I was ready for the clout. Not giving in to AJ's advance, a death grip started with a pop to his side as I pulled him atop of me. "Nice hit."

You'd think it was The Fourth of July, Christmas and your Birthday, the way the Coaches went off. "Yeah, yeah, yeah, yeah!" The plaudits, from both staff and players, were a vindication of my making the team. Quickly, though, three coaches were on

AJ: "Hey AJ. What's the matter? You are stinking up the joint!" I never found out why they gave him such a hard ride: AJ wasn't having any of it.

He just took off his helmet and started walking off the field to the showers. Kids implored him, "Hey AJ...C'mon back" But, AJ would not acknowledge anyone at this time. "C'mon AJ", I yelled out to him a good twenty yards on his slow walk. "C'mon, let's play some ball". He was in his moment to not back down: right here. Relate to it? I made the team.

Once home, the dinner table was not right. I had my sheepish grin give way to my ecstasy to admit that I was playing Freshman ball. Mom smiled - not the resulting dinner conversation I had expected. To ask my Mom what's wrong would be like asking a Russian to play a game of Russian Roulette. My answers would come in due time: a more proper time: so bitter - so slow in its processing. An answer I would later be incapable of perceiving in its truth: "I don't know - I don't know - I just don't know why".

I fell back into what I did know, in the least, understood; Sports.

To complicate matters, though, my 7 1/2 size head led for me to have the ugliest [only] helmet available. We were to practice this time with the Varsity, the team that had some of the toughest players around. It was Wally Toscano, 5'6" with a nasty habit of pummeling his opponents: middle linebacker and had an appearance of being almost as wide as he was tall. Did I mention not an inch of fat on his torso? The scrimmage for our JV team was no Jokeville: in short we were getting down with the worms. "Hey, let's put in Beau....regard", one of the JV coaches said. First play of the second half....coaches said we should be able to get a gain up the middle with some decent blocks. 3 Back off right center....They thought they wouldn't expect this..."BLLLP". Good hand off hole made itself visible, then, the right guard got pushed back and his foot trailed off into the hole. So I began to stumble, forward to making some yards, yet still stumbling. I got to look up there. There was the Cheshire cat grin of the Toz: it was a gleam that linebackers dream of, and I was the recipient. No direction to set and pivot…KAPOW! It was the shot heard 'round the stadium [get up, Rocky}. I was slow to one knee and then came a distorted vision…..purple skies and a blue field…like a used Motorola that had seen too many bad Cowboy movies, my colors were off….Next foot up and I wobbled back to huddle. To say I got my "clock cleaned" was an understatement. I still see Wally today and we laugh as we smoke a cigar. I certainly bolstered his ego when I tell him I had the Van Gogh impression of "Starry Night" implanted by him for some time period [never sure if he knew the artist/ picture yet he still gets a guffaw].

When my brother did come home from college in his freshman-sophomore years, there was a noticeable difference in his bonding efforts with me…We would try to 'get' the first Hendrix album that was the rage of the time: "Are You Experienced". Sex, drugs and Rock and Roll? Not completely off the mark. "Laugh-In" was a put-off for me: "Sock It To Me" came across as a joke. Nehru jackets and color-drawn bodies dancing in cages? I considered this the Madison Avenue trying to cash in on the whole anti-Vietnam War, anti-establishment existing money/ culture. "Fighting the Man" could get argumentative and even sometimes violent. The streets now were not the safe venues for anyone. Mom still had the vision of her sons teaching school. She was in pain more so now. She felt as if she were walking on glass.

I could not put out of my mind that my Mom was sick. She had been diagnosed with Lupus: a strain known a Scleraderma - "Stone Hands" as I was told. Exactly what she was experiencing was as unknown as the disease itself. Penelope, Pop, Chip and I would do our best, but this disease was advanced, slow in its effects and still in its earliest stages. I had realized the value she placed on me when she hobbled around Carson HS as a Security guard where I was student teaching. From the corner of my eye I could see her outside the class with a smile that showed her delight. This was her dream. The co- operating teacher who helped me through all of the rough spots was Tom Perry. Tom

Perry, who took me for long, long walks on off time to try and convince me: "Why do you want to do this to yourself and teach? There are so many things you could do that what would be more rewarding." This was from the most valued teacher of the school! I later figured he was testing my values to be who I had felt destined to become. "You know you'll never get rich by doing this." My Pop had always said that, though: "You were born poor, you're gonna die poor: so you may as well make the best at whatever you choose to do in life". For some reason, I started to think about my Mom and my sister Pin, who was looking forward to her chance at college.

Northern U. and Pipe Heroics

It was the new school opening: Northern U., NJ, or the Vietnam War: CHOICE! A war that my father, who never mentioned his WWII efforts, would emphasize to his two sons: "I don't care what you do, but you are not going to that place for that war." Northern opened one month after school ended and the life raft was gratefully appreciated. No one and I mean educators as well. No one knew what a school of "higher learning" was supposed to be! We were all winging it: the first example of the rustic start was the cow that gave birth on the second day of school just beyond the main entrance, "A Sign". What in the world was their Mission statement? Anti-war protests, Hippie movements of freedom and free love? Protest rallies against the War: protest rallies against the Kent State riots; with a service all free of Psychedelic Spaghetti and tie-dyed t-shirts, and homemade headbands. Students and Professors both spoke out against the war and the means of protest. Woodstock was the path less traveled that the school had accepted for its own personal mantra. My hair: my Mom saw and just could not show her disappointment: but she still understood. Beatles had nothing on my doo, same in length and a curled texture. But, though labeled a hippie by the short-sighted, quick to judge conformists, my response to them was always the same, "It's not the hair, man, it's the head." I had also used the fact that Jesus was a non-violent dissident, a revolutionary.

I set my schedule to fit my classes so I may work at the local Lilymartins supermarket on Route 14 in Lakeside, four days a week at 4:30 until 9pm. All day on Saturday; stocking shelves, pricing and unloading trucks. Classwork and Homework from Northern came at every open opportunity. I had received the State Scholarship to attend college (Both Chipper and I) and I was not going to forget that! The balance worked well for me and my grades never suffered, along with the paycheck. Sunday was the day to "stop and smell the roses", if I wasn't feeling guilty of either of those two venues.

One day, as I was returning from Northern in my cruising' ride: a blue VW Bug, I would witness something that played out as a pivotal moment in my growth as a person. It involved the neighborhood kids playing on these HUGE pipes next door.

Our street had some faulty, failing pipes in the ground that needed to be taken out. These immense pillars were concrete and almost fit the small children playing around them, stacked at least 15 feet high and in a pyramid style. The only thing keeping these pipes together were two copper bands that were expected to keep the temporary structure together. They appeared to be at least 100 pounds each, slanted from a front yard incline. They were nine foot long and at least over 100 pounds each!

As I pulled into the driveway and before I could stop, I saw it.

Kids were slipping off of both sides of the pyramid from climbing as high as they could......the bands had snapped. The hissing sound of "twang" resonated, as kids scattered as fast as breaking a hornet's nest. GONE! As I ran out of the car, I could hear a small child crying, crying for "Help me".

My mind, always active, went blank; I could hardly see a thing but the observed, rolling pillars. I started for the lowest pillar of the once-structure. I would scoop it with both hands and slid it over to one side: but more were on their way: and the crying was no closer.

I heard of these events that people endure all kinds of insane fetes of strength, consciousness absent. This personal "zone-out" put me to a reactive mode: to find the crying child and save him. No thinking, talking, just the strain of these immense pipes that produced a strain that my mind could not handle. Grip, Strain, Angle off, repeat. Can't stop here, the pipes were still in a rolling down mode and they came from the top! Against it…Against it all! To me, this has some form of definition, but why ponder when this is happening. No time to think…and I didn't stop: in a distant fog I could hear my mother imploring me to continue and help as she stood in the front doorway. Who? Is this a sign? No time to think, and there he was just under my feet, as I wedged my body against any further rolling concrete above. A ground imprint from the weight of the pipes and a broken child underneath. Mom called the police and ambulance as the young boy of 4 sat next to me, I caught whatever breath I could and carried him to the front yard of my house. The huge pipes rolled down into the street and clunked and thudded to breaking points.

The sound and mess was continuing…but it was over for me.

He had a broken arm: and I had just learned a different meaning from my Philosophy class on the Myth of Sisyphus: This was no MYTH!

The value of education has never been taken for granted by me. I had tried, sometimes in excess, to share this value in teaching and at home. At home, it would become a reflection upon myself and all that my family had become. At school, variations would create a new set of situations.

Harding offered no new insights for me as the final two-year Odyssey would come to a solemn, yet awkward conclusion. Never fitting in again…Inner city Blues…..I see them come down like the historic "Gabacci," plural for the Frenchy foreigners/ vacationers who visited Spain in the 11th-12th centuries. They were not in particularly happy to be seen: predictable in visual as well as their City accents from New York accents: tattoos abound-Like some millenial from The Illustrated Man: Guinea

T's/tank tops, Banlon Socks, sandals, greased for a fire pit and a haircut that would Peter Maxx blush in its color distortion. "Which way to the Beach" - and be sure to show your figure/muskies! And I? Instead still had the long hair, a guitar, blue Jeans that had seen better days, flannel shirts and a Gaberdine coat : foot length. A severe culture shock for the two of us!

Instead, that deeper knowledge that I sought for myself has dissolved like Alka Seltzer. No call to teach- what a relief it is… NOT! Maybe this was meant for me all along. "Full of Sound and Fury…signifying nothing" [Shakespeare]. The Care packages we got from home were appreciated by all of the frat. Sharing still did not prevent my brother and I to live on the cheap [catsup with some butter and crackers and pepper = Tomato Soup!}

Road Kill Roll

When my brother was ready to get married, we, all of Chip's friends, from college and High School, gathered together to say goodbye to the end of an era. After a night of debauchery that was par for Bachelor Parties, my brother insisted to give me the ride home! His life and mine! Chipper had a white Porsche at this time, though slightly use befit him: the hood down, a dapper hat and scarf. He was a gloried sight. Between holding down his teaching job at David and Goliath HS and summering at home… for him, life was good. I had substituted at his school: Thanks, CB, for getting me in. As we pulled off State Turnpike Exit 213 and into Goliath, across the street from the school parking lot was a figure hanging from a tree by rope! A five pack of Schlitz beer was underneath the figure. "It must be some sort of effigy for the start of the football season."

It was not.

Not my cup of tea to become a teacher: with or without my brother.

Back on the road of the Bachelor night: Chipper had gotten riled up to throw stones at every sign and/or close window to crack or break or express his disdain in this said fashion. I told him, on Route 14, stopped at the Billy-Jo's Diner light, that I wanted to crack the new building window with a stone that was off to the right across the street. He said "no" and, as I leaned forward to throw, he floored the gas on the turn.

Chip didn't notice………. I was no longer in the car… 'WHOOSH'…FLOP, FLOP, FLOP, FLOP……I noticed! After my spinning 'roll' down the Highway my brother was talking to an empty seat AND the door was swinging open. I had gone on a "free roll" for over one hundred feet, ending up across the way from Kokos Car Wash! It was only by the grace of God that there was no one on the road behind me. Road Kill Roll! Just like the sled ride as a kid: I got up in the middle of the Highway as Chipper finally realized he was speaking to his own invisible passenger.

What to say?

LAUGH? OUT LOUD LAUGH!

Mom would wake us up the next morning: "What the hell went on last night? And why is there so much blood on the side of the house?" We both started laughing again….

"I fell

Mom

Substituting for seven years forced me into a second job: a printer/ apprentice at the Mendenhall factory in Farley. Second shift allowed me to work two full time jobs, 7:30 to 3pm and 3:30 to 11pm. My job at Mendenhall job was to power clean the pans that held the red ink for Coca Cola 2 liter wraps: clean again for green on the 2 liter Sprite bottles. A vat containing a mix of cleaning chemicals was used to clean the smaller pans containing said ink.

One time they neglected to tell me that there was a special ink used for the Holiday wraps and that was not to be cleaned in the vat. Unbeknownst to me, I did my routine and a rumble came from the loaded vat: Boom! The vat flew open and the dark muck/caustic soda/ mud and varied chemicals flew up and out...Mostly up, which hit the side of my face and my eyes. I thought me the arch villain of Batman: "Two-Face"....that was going to be me...the 20th Century Phantom of the Opera! There was an eye wash I crawled to as the bubbling could be heard through the section of the factory. Soaking wet, two co-workers helped me to the Medical section. It wasn't too much longer that I decided that 2 full time jobs are one too many.

The way I felt in helping my family out was a vindication. I was throwing two to three hundred dollars on the kitchen table a month: "Pop, this is to help out Mom, I don't want it-won't take it" Proud to the end...... "Then it's for Pin and her going to school: any expenditures she or the house may have". That made it all valid.... I knew whatever it was that I needed was nothing compared to the needs of Mom.

The Scleraderma had reached her hands, legs and most importantly, her lungs. It was the sobs of pains that echoed the quiet halls at night, from my parents' bedroom that had me quietly as possible, put on my clothes and sneak out the back door to a bar so that I can deal with the pain. Sometimes it was until last call, sometimes I stayed all night: dozing to the rhythm of the waves, breaking all night: the roll and rumble made for a lessening of the stress I felt. Sleep: it's a righteous thing.

Mom's ulcerations advanced beyond her hands to her feet and bed soars on her back. I would try to help her by cleaning/ carrying her to a wheelchair or to the commode. Once she surprised me and clasped her arms onto mine as I carried her back to bed. I heard the pop and felt the fluids dripping down my arms as my mother exclaimed: "I'm sorry, Ozzie...please, I'm sorry....They were bothering your mother so much." "It's OK, Mom, it's OK." I turned and walked away in a faint to the bathroom to disguise my shame.

Her blisters were gone, not the pain.

I knew I had reached my limits: but they were mine to own: and no one else.

Pop had Mom sent to the hospital, against her wishes: the bedroom stench was awful...I don't know how Penelope did as much as she had done. Gangrene had set in on my Mom's legs and the Medical unit burst in to take charge: Straight to the bedroom. "I don't want to go, Daddy, Daddy, don't do this, I want to stay with you!" The unit wrapped her in a clean sheet and hoisted her up above their heads to get through the hallway. "Ozzie, don't let them do this, please don't let them take me away from you...I love you." What could I do?...I could only stare at the Cross at the end of the hall. Pop went in the ambulance and the doctor sat on our front porch. He said there was no cure...."you did everything you humanly could for my Mom." Have no idea why I felt I needed to comfort a doctor. Awkward.

It was 6 months of soul searching.

"Look what I can do" my Mom said, as she raised her two stumps that were once legs and scissored them in the air. "I still can feel my toes, too". This was the moment of empathy that I consider necessary for all teachers to have/need. If it could be bottled, it would make millions: If it could be taught, a whole new concept for Education would be processed, then again most likely, again, bottled. Bandaged and drugged but not in pain... Yet my Mom was slowly losing her essence of being Mom... Scabs and ulcers spread and her mind went, as her eyes twisted to the outside corners: She became virtually comatose. I tried to tell her, "I'm sorry if I caused any of this...I never had the chance to say it and I hope God allows you to hear that I love you". It was so difficult to kiss her Goodbye.

Pin had said her time was coming: if I wanted to see her, do so that day.....She died in September, 3 weeks later. This is not the lasting memory I sought to keep.

I broke down at the funeral parlor...Everyone asked, "Was it timely?" I wasn't going to lie. This was not the same person I played ball with, watching Chip, Pin and I rip open presents on the couch at Christmas. I gave her a first Mom's Day flowers..... pansies-when I was nine. I watched as my father just.....left....

left everyone rather than come home to explain or listen to the condolences ad nausea: his destination unknown to this day. I was inconsolable.

This was one rock that I would not wish upon anyone: to "hold on" is all.

I could only work: work and work. Two jobs became five, Subbing, Wrestling coach at a local HS and Sutters Senior counselor at Camp, working the bar and the door at a small but efficient Tooleys bar, raking leaves and cutting lawns and delivering the Sunday paper at Saturday night to 5AM Sunday morning. Keep busy..so busy...Too busy. Self-pity is selfish...you can dwell on your crybaby attitude later.

I also became a transient, into a trailer park, in Florida. One place led to another...... a third place, . As the moves ended out of state ..... I had lived in a frat house, into a trailer park where I substituted, sold cable TV and served as a waiter at a nearby Tennis & Golf resort. The job market was there, but for how long, who could tell? My next door neighbor demanded that I give back the parking space next to my place... but he still claimed it for his truck. "Hi Neighbor". Summer came, the sidewalks were pulled in. No further subbing and sales were saturated: the Resort got too hot. The work, too cold.

As fate would have it, things got uglier; when my less-than congenial neighbor came out one night with a concrete wheel to sharpen his imposingly long knife! He made it more than known that "snow birds" are not welcome in his part of HIS County........

I was home in a day: I had five dollars to my name.

Return of the Penguin

I had been substituting for eight years. A long time to push the rock. Yet, there was no other recourse. A degree in teaching Social Studies? In which direction can one branch out? Maybe the Library or Social Work. Substituting in different districts was my only way to come close to a decent living, that and any other work.

I came back home to find out my sister had married and given birth! My Pop was silent; I can only imagine what was going through his mind. I was homeless and had already played the nomad role.... out of my car, slept on the beach, car or anyone who offered shelter, which were few. When the full time job for Burnside opened up, I was ecstatic! Atonement! It is in order here! A sign, possibly from God, as a return of the native son.... where it all began. God truly has a place for those less fortunate! He has seen......

The Administrative Principal and Vice Principal were both nuns. It didn't surprise me: in fact it was anticipated as part of my ordeal ahead. No Gimmicks here! Though I was asked and I turned down the position of track coach for girls, I did take the wrestling and baseball jobs. It was too soon for them to be disappointed: but they were, though. I was coaching and teaching for half of what a public school teacher makes. I was ready to do anything necessary to keep this position. Up until the morning hours to prep for the AP World class and US I classes I taught. The day of Reckoning came early in the first semester: to observe all new teachers. I prepped and prepped for this lesson.

I did not prep the students....BIG Mistake. An Arrogance of Ignorance?

As the VP sat in the back of the room of the US II class, forget any "Good Mornings" or even an acknowledgment that she had entered, I began the class regardless. Students knew of the ulterior motive of the "visitor". Had I proposed that it was the class being observed; maybe the outcome would have been different. The nun was primed and writing frantically as I went on with my lesson....Intimidating.

Nevertheless I ignored the steely-eyed glares I received and the feverish pitch to which she was writing, as if it were a vision to document! The class was mildly berated by me when I asked a question to 2-3 students that regarded their Homework from the previous day: "How can you learn anything in this class by not doing the Homework expected of you? You'd better come out of the closet and start doing these assignments".

The nun's reaction was like a powder keg-she was pushing her pen so fast, it was like a buttered knife. Class ended. "Meet me after class, Mr. Beauregardi".

Truman Capote's last written words: *"More tears are shed over answered prayers, than unanswered ones."*

As if it were practiced in a mirror, the nun's expression was one of severe disdain. My first thoughts were of Dante's Inferno, with a Divine Retribution pointing to my soul. Then, I thought it out: what was wrong now: a return from earlier times?: So necessary for me to defend my actions in class?

"Mr Beauregardi; Did you or did you not tell your students to "come out of the closet"? I was back in third grade: "Yes, Sister". "Do you understand that type of commentary is totally inappropriate for a parochial school?" The closet? "Do you understand what that means?" "I don't know sister,: A room for clothes, coats and shoes and the like?"

IRATE…her face turned a red as Grandpa's Borscht. Then my AHA moment came in the midst of her fury: I was about to be arguing with a nun over SEX! Sex and Homosexuality…..
Her seriousness over these interpreted comments… Frightening! No way was there to engage in this controversy.

A no-win situation. But I didn't need to sell my soul to work!

My faith was MINE, so I apologized for my ignorance and swore it would never happen again [familiar?]….The remainder of my contract had a Bulls-eye on my back, while the VP nun had actually danced in the Church in front of the new teachers. Every minute detail was examined and re-examined: her pen was gripped like the sword of Damocles….her tabloid was out on me…Me…The Stepford Teacher!

At the end of the year there was an evaluation held in private for every teacher [mostly new] who had the luxury of a firing line of questions to validate their place in Burnside for the next year. Past transgressions, fresh in my mind….. had me, similar to the sickness that my Mother endured…to a point of no return. I knew as a first year teacher I was expendable, and, when I sat down, the Principal and Vice Principal nuns were as grim in face as they were stoic. This was not the ideal moment to be asking for a raise.…The VP had a stack of folders ready to introduce, to warrant her "valid" concerns over hiring me for the next year. Immediate flash: A perfect venue for one to bargain faith for employment? Wasn't this an indulgence of the pre-Reformation? Times maybe have not changed much at all! Wasn't this first year hard enough? Do I need this struggle again? The Rock, Oscar.… regrip and understand the next push.

"What did you think of your first year at our school, Mr. Beau regardi?" One thing I had learned in schools' constant confrontations, especially as a sub, is never to go into the jungle with the animals. I expressed what I considered my credible job as the new AP World teacher and not only had we won a third place trophy for a first year ever Freshman baseball team: We also won a Christmas Wrestling tournament with a half of a squad, practicing on Christmas Day!

"Excuse me," blurted the VP nun…"but I have some incidents that I would care to".…and THAT was the moment.…. The moment of instantaneous clarity:

"Excuse me, sister" in my interjection to her portfolio-reading.…Grandpa's snapping the chicken who had pecks on my head. "I feel that it is in the best of all concerned, that I inform you I have no intention of returning next year to my position here to teach; I have learned a very great deal here and I appreciative the opportunity."

"But I have it here, right here that…"

"In all due respect, sister, I would like to finish {WHOA}… I've given the students here the very best education that I could: this I know and assure you… It is still, as it appears to me, that I have not met the expectations that you expected of me. So, out of respect of the position as well as my faith, I will complete my contractual obligations until the end of the school year." Silence.

Prolonged….After a half minute of this…. I stood to walk out, no objections from the 2 nuns, Silence permeates…. I then did a deliberate slow walk away, not run, and NOT with a Beanie on my head….

I turned around and said "I know when I am not wanted". I walked out.

"You Cannot Petition the Lord with Prayer" (Soft Parade: the Doors) Deja vu

Tai Chi in Class

I've seen Van Gogh colors in the sky,
on an autumn afternoon.

A Palace with a long Hall of Mirrors
and a broken mirror in a trailer park home.

Served Crepe in a Parisian Bistro
and Croc at an Outback billabong.

Saw a man panhandle with a 2 string Mandolin
with a pair of Nikes sitting next to him.

The Barrier Reef as a Paradise
and a grave of a rock hero at an unknown site

I met worlds where its people were the finest exports
and poor, seeking deposit for an unfinished water bottle.

Seeking any port.

I have yet to decide if our world truly demands Arrogance
or is there a distance from the legacy of Ignorance.

1. 392 steps of the Sun Yat-sen Mausoleum, Nanjing, China are not visible the top

2. The city of Nanjing (background)is engulfed in a "fog"

3. The Emperor's private lake and waterfall

4. Southern California State
a. Koy fish: very friendly

5. Southern California Harbor showing the "haunted"
   Queen Mary and a submarine of dubious location

6. Australian

a. kangaroo at lunch; Townsend Zoo (Made a purchase of
   a 'Canned Koala')

b. Sydney Olympic site: workers sang "Waltzing Matilda"...I sang "America the Beautiful"

7. Notre Dame Cathedral Eiffel tower and the obscure burial place of Jim Morrison

PART 2
ENVIRONMENT
("It's amazing how complete is the delusion that beauty is goodness") Tolstoy

Old and New Times

My best years as a teacher: both substituting and contractual-have today swung to a living in the past. That living has taken away some of my humility.......... every day, a little more subtraction. Yet, it was Lincoln who I paraphrase: "It's not the work that you do in life, rather the life you put into your work".

With all of the 'events' experienced through my years involving my faith and the Church, the first feelings I get remind me of the Movie where a Nazi trooper slowly presses his bayonet, by hand into the GI while imploring him face-to-face in this final act; "SSHHHHHHHH" ("Saving Private Ryan"). Guilt - That frailty that makes cowards of us all. More than just a tear, it shames me that my mother could be looking down on me saying: "It's alright Ruby-Doo; it wasn't meant to be; you're better off without them; God has a greater plan for you". She had seen my student teaching, but never teaching my own class. My sister called to say the same thing: "Don't worry about them….It wasn't in God's plans…You never know what could happen, with all that grief you would have to endure." What great support I had! Maybe there's some type of mathematical probability that is involved in all this: If you keep betting red at the Roulette wheel and it stays on black, the next time, does red have a better chance of showing up? Maybe I just haven't paid all my dues yet. It feels better when you've pounded and pounded your head against the wall….and stop. School became this for me.….Push the Rock. But, after 10 years of substituting throughout the County area: It was Lagrand… Lagrand Schools hired me: without fanfare or politics. THEY WANTED ME!

The interview for Lagrand was with a man who I only remember as "Sid". I had filled in for a retiring teacher for substitute pay: He had been showing US History clips from the none-too familiar-Dukane Projector. His parting words to me were "Just be cool".

The man I today called the "Saint Thomas", Tom Donahue, spoke to me as well as spoke up to my being hired. It was Christmas vacation and the job became mine for the beginning of 1985. Ten years at the rock: Did you see me, Mom?

Like a retreaded tire, I had searched for work: regroup and non-stop. As if I was being hoodwinked.….Too good to be true. The Selling of indulgences: a price I still needed to pay. Hereditary? I am hoping all that I have learned, grown to live and believe-that I had yet to meet my potential. Round and round we go: It's not what you know…. but who. Lagrand hired me regardless….OUCH! Isn't this a counter-revelation! *"When something goes right, it's apt to confuse me"* [Paul Simon].

I still say my morning prayers ... in the cold of January, pleading for my family to be safe and happy. I know never to put all my eggs in one basket, but like Easter: the competition for eggs was never fair. Not today, Never. I had always found work as a younger man, whether cleaning toilets or raking leaves, cutting lawns, coaching wrestling or baseball, working the door of a bar, delivering newspapers, dig holes for pools with my brother or substituting. Work was my answer to all things. There was once a time all things were possible. Validation through work ethic. I counted myself as one of the lucky ones, now. It ran like a blur: faster and less clear than the Dukane: lesson plans/

attendance/class control. These were my mid-year (January), first year of teaching.

Today's different: Anyone tells you that there is no age discrimination in this country, just send them to me...The local supermarket won't even higher me. Do I need to expound upon this? A Master's degree in Education and I can't even shelve canned peaches? I do pity those who are expecting large pensions or even a decent Social Security payment after they worked for so many years. These millennial/Elite-ists are showing the arrogance of ignorance: they are "in for a penny - in for a pound".....or should I say "Pounding": Living for the moment in a virtual reality world and texting until their debts finally meets its self-centered "soul mate', there can be no recourse for them but to keep working, or become a textoid: a less-than-model citizen for their children to look upon. Children who never question whether the world was always like this. Lazy, quick to temper, "the world owes me a living" and "I deserve it: now": no empathy or regards of kindness, nor respect.

And most likely no Social Security nor Pension to look forward to. A future too bleak to comment.

"Why you sneakin' me, cuz?" a student would ask me. "Why you cuzzin me, sneak?" my quip of a response.

"Why don't you take a chill pill, Mr Beau?"

"Why? Who is the illin', since you not be willin' as you provin your word has no skillin'.....just.......WORD!

WORD IS BOND...JAMES BOND...OH SNAP OH JUNK OH EBONICS"...and now.............the pause for effect.............

"Once again, Mr Beauregardi has failed to live up to the expectations of a 16 - year - old."

"Hey man, I'm 17!"

.... and there you are.

"I GOT A BIG FAT "F" FOR YOUR REFRIGERATOOOOOR....MMMMM-Bop-de-Bop

All you want to do is sit and fail....
You'll eat out of the garbage pail!
Big Fat "F" for your Refrigerator....MMMMMM-Bop-Bop.

All denominations, gender and creeds are acting out this way (by my experiences)....After a while, it becomes mundane! "Just give me a passin' grade and I'm outta this....hole": and back to texting or sleeping, or talking in a loud manner to someone across the room: "Notice me while I perform my defiance to authority by being a social ingrate" attitude.. . A total disregard to anyone wishing to learn. But there are some, some who care: who will speak up and admonish these A of I-s: "Hey Tina, why don't you just shut the .....up ; Nobody cares about your weekend, or how hot you think Pedro is...." Nice to hear; Sometimes I let the parents know of these things [...No, not Tina's, but the other person], who spoke up for herself, others, and myself! Phone:

"Mrs. Jones, This is Mr Beauregardi at the High School: WAIT !!! Let's not jump to any conclusions on your daughter! I thought you would like to know about something I considered outstanding she did in class...You did a very nice job bringing her up, if I may be so honest with you, as a parent as well as a teacher." Parents need support, too. I was never one too bashful to go to the phone to let the parent know what was going on.... good or bad, even while class was in session! I knew I would appreciate a call if and when ANYTHING was happening with my kids at school. CALL ME!

"Mr. B, you are so ANNOOYYYING......"

"Mean Mr. Beau sleeps in the park, shaves in the dark, tries to save paper........." (Beatles : Mean Mr Mustard)

"IT WAS THE BEST OF TIMES...."

Considering all of the events that made me who I am, I can't help but to refer back to my days of studying Sisyphus: Philosophy class at Northern U. pushing a rock that I chose. Maybe it wasn't large enough, considering Education: perhaps the incline was too easy.

That would be pitiful! I often wonder if I had reached my pinnacle too early, imparting experiences personal as well as academic, wherever I go today: to the local market, the doctors, out with my brother (to whom I once shared a Cain and Abel relationship): all who I would have contact with...pathetic? Is it possible that this teacher attempted to reach something that was never meant to be ? Who has made a difference in this world: and what, if anything can I assume the world will think of ME? Which of my students: which of them will be the next Gandhi, Lincoln, Malcolm X lest I leave out Mother Teresa, Florence Nightingale and countless others who were capable of suppressing the hateful elements that develop in our society today?

This thinking makes me a failure; predictably so by my standards, even if no one can be perfect! These distorted-thoughts.....Do they make me unworthy of the position I held? I keep telling myself that we can't always be at our best: yet this is a learning environment we exist in, with the hopes and aspirations that we encounter in our daily lives.

A dichotomy: much the same as the title above: The Russia and US Cold War, National Security vs. the rights of the individual, a Puritan work ethic vs. the "its not what you know, but who you know", teaching with innovation and creativity vs. the core curriculum standards mandate : according to the "No Child Left Behind" Act. The rock that I push seems to roll back down and to continue through a repeated process -over and over and over again. Is it truly an absurd life we live? If it is true that we can always learn something... any one thing, maybe this is it! Sisyphus had it right: his knowledge - what he did, a farmer, cheating death twice as he walks back down the mountain to start again his arduous, valueless life, he knew: and probably still does....... his self- determination, forever/fate he accepted because of a life he had lived: within these memories-he is happy. I believe all of us have a rock; some baggage/memory/struggle that we have by happen chance, chosen by us to reach some personal accomplishment. The size of said rock, its weight, is only for that individual to choose.

The Pushing, the efforts one places to their task: shoulder to the stone, hold, grip and drive forward: only to re grip and start the process again. The incline is the time one puts into this effort....no stopping or resting. This is the New Puritan work ethic, where, unlike Sisyphus, there exists a small but recognizable victory: one that does NOT need recognition. Satisfaction in a job well done! One has problems today recognizing this ever existing!

Even this appears to be a dichotomy to me. My mother always said I could be whatever I wanted to be: and she spent her dying days with a belief that I was going to be a great teacher: I believed it myself. My Mother never did get that opportunity to see her son be what some may claim as a success: Her last words of any coherence to me; in confidence: "I feel so sorry for you Ozzie; you are going to have such a hard time". I feel this was not the truest statement: though living in a struggling family, having a brother whose empathy comes forward as my mentor/ helper, he had grown to become a great teacher; a sister whose sounding board and sage advice had become a matriarch for the family. Without Pin, the family would be a nomadic travesty: wandering and hiding our little secrets: and the students, the ones who come back at a moments' notice, to not only recognize, but to thank me for insights and efforts as the teacher of their class giving them a valuable jewel to keep forever . Never once was I given the "notoriety" of being selected by my peers as the Teacher of the Year, or even the month! I slept well every night. The barometer of a teacher who had a great day and I revel in this. By "bowing to every teacher recognized" as "of the Month" or "Year".....

"Stop everything....BOW...We are NOT WORTHY". One can come to many conclusions....But I never needed that recognition/conclusion: when you know what you are doing is the right thing...this is why I had never bothered to observe other teachers... I had a never - doubt confidence to do what was demanded: to meet the needs and provide my best efforts.

Maybe it is a right to question - maybe it was the drive to give as much as possible in a 90 minute period what students need to know in class as well as life: A perfect example of this, showing the assassination of JFK when the World History class could hardly reach that time period (for how much history of the World can one cover?). It was amazing to me how many students never knew of the controversies that surrounded that historic event: never saw the Zapruder tape.

How can any teacher let that piece of history just go by and neglect its moral implications: effecting so many lives for generations!? In that 90 minutes of Bloc scheduling, I would lecture the whole time....and when the bell rang to leave, the students were still glued to their seats to find out more... ... "What? No you can't leave now! The best part of all this is ...." and they are gone to the next class, but some, a few with the inquisitive "AHA" moment : they still remained behind.....Did the Tudor family really have that royal 'strangeness' to it ? Historically, are they the only ones? Was the French Revolution an after effect of the English and American Revolutions? Did Columbus really discover America? What if Zheng He turned left, instead of right? How could Hong Xiu Quan, calling himself Jesus' younger brother, create a "Heavenly Kingdom" and conquer such a wide expanse of China in the 1840s-1850s - killing 100's of millions of people.

No Child Left Behind? How about no stone left unturned? And are we doing students any "favors" by pushing them out!?

I remember finding out, through a lesson of Dante's Inferno in one of my World classes, using the creative insights that a young High school student may have (later chapter). A new Hell with (as many they would consider) "sinful" levels of "Circles" that show society today. They have in their determination, a personal stake in this! If a student had put a teacher's name in one of the steps of Hell: how could this happen? I approached the students' with the information confided to me: that said student(s) had been abused by an earlier year teacher who was thought was, well, a trusted confidante.

Needless to say, I approached the Guidance Office with this information, as well as the principal: following protocol. Yes, I did not sleep too well that night, even though what was necessary and proper was done. Does Congress still exercise that "Elastic Clause"?

First Day "Tourniquet"

As if I were a student again to look for a grade, I always kept, in the back of my mind, how the student was going to grade me! Hypocritical, in that its essentially only a number that someone is rating you on a selected criteria. Every year I gave the students 5 questions to answer grading me as their teacher, without signing their names: recommended for new teacher: This is in a later section [some feel that the anonymity wasn't enough, for, as their teacher, "You know our handwriting"]. Here, I must mention that script has been abandoned by the powers that be in the learning process at primary schools; seeing it more necessary to deal with other projected tasks that may assist students in later life. In any event: the 5 Questions:

1. What do you like best about this class?
2. What do you like least about this class?
3. On a scale of 1 to 10. 10 highest I give Mr Beauregardi a.......
4. Because.............
5. The one thing I'd like to tell Mr Beauregardi is.......

It was my last year teaching that I had scored my only C (83) out of the 28 years doing this: always A's and sometimes a few B's [adding the answers to question 3 and divide by the number of students}.

Maybe I had gone far enough in education: in pushing the rock...yet the fire still burns to educate to impart knowledge: never to abandon those willing to learn and become accountable for the actions one does in life. Is it possible that in the sufferings I witnessed in my years has made me a better person, or maybe even a better teacher? Who is it that says, "If it doesn't kill you, it makes you stronger"?

So we can't always be the best teacher: no such thing as perfection. But the accountability is YOURS as an individual.

Grading teachers is a great tool to use for readjustment. Example: student would ask for "More Jeopardy and less Homework". One does not need to be ignorant of the anonymous statements made by students. But they do give direction: a direction that the students will recognize as their opinions COUNT.

Picking your "moments" to glimpse at the eternal: the "AHA" moment. And you will know it when it happens, for no one needs to give you plaudits when your efforts bear the fruit always known by you to exist!

On that first day, as the class would enter, I waited outside until the late bell rang.....I would wait another minute, a long awkward minute: still waiting outside the class until the students had settled into their positions without a teacher. I had answered no questions said nothing during this time: I just waited.

I walked into the class with a 'Good Morning, class". Note/realize I had earlier put my name on the Board: they also knew the classroom/class and teacher name by their Guidance admission slip.

Still, no response.

I would turn around and exit the class, my back turned to them, then swiftly turned back, standing at the doorway with a slow, deliberate walk to match my next words: "Let's try this again, LEST we have HOMEWORK." There's that familiar mumble-grumble..Fait accompli...."Good Morning, class"....

"Good Morning Mr. Beauregardi".

Your very first lesson in this class: Good manners are, or maybe I should say are not... taught in this class. This common courtesy should have been in you before you have entered ANY class. Do I really need to take away from your academic time for what "common decency" is? Regardless of anything that I am saying at this point, as important as I may consider it: No Homework takes top honors. Silly, Absurd, Ridiculous;

Effective.

I now turned to the Board and wrote the following quote, used for as many years as I would remember it:

"Failure…(and a long pause to make for an effective first day) is the condiment for the flavor of success". Truman Capote "Can anyone tell me what this means?" Silence…Keep the tourniquet on…." what is a "condiment?" By this time students are answering…of course it takes patience and a few right-wrong suggestions. "To be successful, one must accept and learn to recognize failure. There is an old saying that 'When you beat your head up against a wall, it feels better when you stop'; When you add a taste to that recognized failure, you are on the path of not continuing that head-bashing. You have started to think, outside of the box and are searching for a different way to answer for YOUR success".'

Or is it all just Mean Mr. Mustard?

If you find yourself with that head against the wall situation, trying every avenue to come to a logical conclusion, then it is time to ask for help. A clue/hint and you'll see that to know what you know what you don't know, you are on your way of knowing it".

It's the work ethic…some called it the Puritan work ethic that you will recognize and hopefully have when you leave this class. One that will allow you to make your own choices in school/ job/even life! If you have no choices, then someone or thing has made that for you…..No Choices means that your freedom to be has been compromised….Ergo, CHOICE IS FREEDOM.

Then I would throw another witty-ditty at them…."And this is not just fact, but truth!" Some may think I just opened Pandora's box {not the sound system!}. There it is…. the hand raised with the most obvious but still expected question:"

"Mr Beauregardi? What's the difference"…"Anyone venture a guess? Or do you get made fun of if you give a wrong or silly, by 'their peers' standards, answer. Bullying, even in mocking another student has no place here. I expect any and all questions! If you don't ask, won't that head of yours start to bang, even in indifference: a blissful ignorance? If you don't ask, you won't find out.

Fact vs Truth…This is a chair… I stand here…you sit there [for today]…but Truth is what you believe!!!! And that is why history has so many faiths: what is Belief is yours! Not just religion, but the choice is freedom what you have chosen to believe to be true!

Whew! A great exhaust permeates the class…This place is going to be different…You better believe it, Gabacci!

If you don't ask-you don't get an answer.

"Hand raised"…

"Hey Mr. Beauregardi, what about late to class?"

"Excellent question" I forgot to cover: "Allow for me to demonstrate what I would see and determine as your question begs an answer…I step outside the classroom where I was at the beginning of class….and, outside in the hallway I hear 'Yo, man, I'll see you later for lunch. I got Mr B., so I don't have to worry about him: he and I are as close as two peas in a Pod d….[entrance of late student]….Yo, You know I was held up and, I know your my main man…like, I had something that needed my attention and….

STOP.. RIGHT THERE

"[from the movie of the same name] Stand and Deliver!

"What you talking about man?

"Stand right where you are, no, no seat, and explain to the class why they need to come to class on time and you don't… And please… Address them, not I, because they understood the value of being present for class and made the effort to be in class at the appointed time." After some mumbling and fumbling, the students in class are instructed: : "What punishment, if any, do you feel this individual needs?" Every time it would be something more harsh than anything I would give: "2 days detention….. after school detention for a week…..send him to the office." Something more lenient would be assigned for this, the first time.

Firm but fair.

" ...And The Worst of Times"

It would not be fair for me to expound on the good events/things that had happened in my life without mentioning my faults. Oh yes, I am as human as anyone and I most definitely do not want the reader to believe that I am a braggart. There is no Saint here: to this I admit my "arrogance", if the reader determines it so.

Mia culpa...Mia culpa...Mia maxima culpa

"The faults lie not in the stars, my dear Brutus, but in ourselves (" Julius Caesar")" This was the last quote I gave the Board of Education when I was called in to be held accountable for my actions in my last year as a teacher. Two events had happened: Both within a period of less than two weeks. There but by the grace of God.......

The first one was my blocking of a doorway preventing a student who had abruptly left her seat to grab some candy from her beckoning friend, outside the classroom: a friend who had already been removed from my class earlier in the year for walking out of class for no apparent reason.....just stood up and walked out ("Excuse me...Where are you going? Please sit back down"). She had been transferred out. A few days later, there she is, at my doorway. I ignored her, to continue the lesson and not give any credence to what she was up to - she did not knock - just motioning with a bag of candy. A seated student-friend abruptly stood up and asked to go to the bathroom: it does not take a rocket scientist to figure two plus two: her wish was denied. Knowing this was to be a set-uptake the teacher look foolish, I had TEN TIMES [yes, I counted] to sit back down. She turned back to her seat, but then, turned quickly toward the door: the Bum's Rush, as if to "make a break for it". Tootsie Roll pops were the "it". I blocked the doorway and held the handle; the girl pushed, elbowed and nudged me as I was attempting to call for a hall guard through a partially opened door.. The whole thing must have appeared comical. She then asked to go to the office, to which I gave the "OK". GONE...."Well, that was interesting - but some pleasantries should go unnoticed" and the lesson continued. The story was presented to the office, I could only imagine: The results were not in my favor (as if) as I was reprimanded for preventing a student from leaving the class . I told my side to the administrator. I was to receive another letter of reprimand for inappropriate conduct; regardless of the physical actions: Assault, against me, in the doorway. To note, the camera in the room ("installed for the teachers' safety") was right underneath us, so no eye witnessing took place. No one; not a teacher, student, hall-guard, administrator saw a thing. No one heard a thing. Blind justice in an Alien-nation.

The second was my actually trying to help the most overworked, underpaid employees of the school: the Hall guards. During lunch, one guard/aide had to go to the rest room: I said I would watch his position-outside the cafeteria for the time he needed. Two students from the cafeteria asked to go see a teacher for some help in a subject: an immediate dilemma, for neither student had a pass from said teacher. "We always go" was their explanation. I was always told to demand a pass to keep the hallways clear, particularly during the lunch periods. They demanded to go and I rejected them: "Who is your Teacher?" I had asked. They looked at me quizzically: "Do you need me to spell that out? T-E-A-C-H-E-R".

They were of another heritage, ESL, yet I wasn't aware of this -nor did I look for it. They also failed to realize I had seen them numerous times in the hallway, wandering about on my floor, munching on those highly nutritious saggy bags of chips, enjoying their own personal walk through the park/hall. I knew what the protocol was. That was my Modus Operandi. An administrator had been there, behind me, in his office: I SAW HIM HIDE TOWARD THE BACK OFFICE: nothing done for assistance. Not only was I sent to the principal's office, I was sent another letter: This time not only a reprimand, but to report and confront the Board of Education for a deposition, explaining my actions: one should know better than to spell out words to any student..... This other "event" was added to my meeting with the Board of Education.

It was in the next two weeks that I would be summoned to the Board concerning my contract. My fellow workers had avoided me like the plague - wordless, zero support. My Union at work.....On the appointed evening, resolved myself to walk in to the Board Office, my job on the line. Like most bureaucracies one is expected to wait. And I waited..... For what seems as an eternity: a thin vestibule, with the school principal on one side of me and the administrator on the other. I remained motionless and mute between them, facing ahead for my fate. I could smell the cheap after shave from my left, and the seeping overuse of Ode de Gabacci from my right. Worse was their cold insignificance towards me: they appeared annoyed to be there. They still were not as uncomfortable as I. Yet I felt firm in my resolve to be facing the same people who had given me the opportunity to be what I had desired to be. The faces though, had changed; for their time came and went. Was the same to be expected for me?

To the best of my memory, I had first thanked the Board who had hired me after ten years of substituting in Lagrand County area. They hired me on merit and not by any infamous nepotism that permeates our world of work today. "Who I know" was no one at that time...No one. I then used my Julius Caesar quote. I followed this with a request, a move that I saw heads turn (app 40+ people in a timed-calculated 90 degree turn) as if they had been rudely awoken: I asked for one more year in the classroom ......to complete my work and give back to the school that was first to hire me. I felt I should lay all of my cards on the table: as if I was to call, or raise the stakes, or just hold. I made it my call, not theirs! I told the members present I just needed one more year to be able to take care of my family.... A clear; "Oh Please"........... abrupted my address, from a distant side seat that had a view of the whole proceeding: an administrator, (who I did not recognize) who was sitting off and to the right that had been in the vestibule. I would not acknowledge her, keeping true to my task and its importance. I continued and thanked them again. No questions were asked of me. Silence was less than golden-that "deafening sound"....I can attest, it truly exists. My words had fallen to deaf ears - hardly an ideal situation, for their minds had been decided earlier.

It was all foreshadowing. "Whatever you said", Paul, the lone representative from the Union, who was with me for moral support, mentioned outside the room that I probably spoke "over their heads" and they had already made a consensus decision, before I even entered.

"the time has come," the Walrus said "to speak of many things
Of ships and sail and sealing wax
Of cabbages and Kings" [the Walrus and the Carpenter]
Paul was my confidante when I was a Guidance Counselor for two years at the Valory Elementary School. I saw too many things happening to little children that I, at one time, thought I could help. After too many unanswered DYFS calls and the true "wire hanger" and cigarette burns witnessed, my mind was an overcooked omelet! I did get to see the same students graduate High School....they smiled a smile of self-reliance.

I thought I was to the point. I wonder today what they thought when I started with "I have a propensity to be verbose"! Deafening silence, I knew: Call it an inclination or a premonition: their minds were already made up. When you bang your head against the wall too many times, doesn't it feel better to stop? "Deus Volt": it is God's will.

I completed my school year with my Social Security and Pension intact. I miss teaching.

Maybe, just another premonition, there is more than just a Tale of TWO "Cities". A Dichotomy could have been a Trichotemy, perhaps even more. There were the following "players" in my final years as a teacher:

A. The teacher as a "professional" determined through many changing vari An auto-tron in fear of being fired. Pull the right strings and your desired r will result.
B. The so-many different students with

   a. Social
   b. Economic
   c. Ethnic/ethical differences that make for a more than just disjointed culture today-aka "baggage"? A great scapegoat for any connected problem? Guess!

C. "He's over salaried".
D. The Parents, who have their own per-conceived ideologies of what educati their school should be: what the School decides must be the best for all of us.

So many variables…. I feel sure I have forgotten some: Still the school is to make whole this amalgamated hodgepodge of differences into one cohesive learning environment. Who determines how this great puzzle is to fit: becoming a school that all would wish to attend? And who determines what that picture - if any, is? Any one of the above? The State Department of Education? The Federal Government with its own 50 - state complexities toward what makes a student prepared for the outside world? Standardized testing? Who is in favor of that? Raise your hand!

When these moments of 'twisting in the wind' problems reach me, I have a memory of pushing those huge concrete pipes years ago: the snapping of its copper bindings under the weight of the children playing on top, and, under the immense weight, burying a 4 year old underneath: crying for help. I can still hear my mother in a haze from the front door: "Oscar! You've got to do this: please keep going….you have to help him". My mind blanks out as the voice of my mother trails off beyond my coherence - I heard nothing but the child's cries and my grunting-exertion. It was as if a trance-like Odyssey given to me; alone and nothing but a sheer effort for support against those 50+ cylindrical monoliths.

School: A great 'structure': A pyramid, perchance? Like Rome…

I would often think of moments at school, when trouble evolved: this was on a daily basis. How much support existed when I had found the task to endure far too much for one…. and then, what of the newer teachers? They had to feel intimidated and afraid to involve themselves with an altercation that "demanded" their attention. Don't stir the hornet's nest! Lee Marvin in "The Wild Ones": "Oh, the shame of it all…call my Mom".

No teacher claims to ever be aware of the Lolly pop kid or the 2 students seeking their own mini-vacation/picnic. "I didn't hear anything……., I was too busy…. into my lecture……I was busy……I was out. ….I never realized it". I thought my fellow teachers had my back. They were really covering their own.

Push that stone Oscar, there IS a purpose to it!

This is the arrogance of MY ignorance.

A New Lost Generation: Tricks

"Never underestimate a man who overestimates" (Warren Buffett).

The value of a teacher CANNOT be measured by the number of students who pass a class. I know of many teachers who avoid the annoyance and headaches, along with the extra work given when a student is failing for the year. Extra work and no extra pay…..Unions - parents - administrators - teachers: Who wants to play the Blame Game? Education is ill. Can All the blame be on the teachers?

This last winter, my brother and I went out to find coins with a couple of contraptions that beep through the sand to allow one to find various artifacts: much like the early scientists seeking the levels of civilizations along tells. Fishing on land is more of what we were doing…. in Mid - January. The sand was mostly too hard to sift through.

My first find, a dime. "Now I can go to the racetrack."

"Hey, that can be a ten-cent Superfecta bet" . My Bro... Always thinking.

If you heard of Beginner's luck, that was it : I was 'hozed, screwed, nailed and juiced' by an unforgiving beach. I won't elaborate on these findings, but a hardware shop would not be out of the equation at that moment.

After speaking to one of my graduated students, my new boss, who just happens to be working at the caregiver job I now hold as part-time; she told me "Thank you for all of your advice and help". I found myself befuddled - not knowing how to respond: getting a plaudit is so out of the ordinary, though not really anticipated for a retired teacher (let alone ANY teacher). Caught off guard, I gave the pat answer," It wasn't me; it was your parents who drove you into the position you find yourself in today". As an afterthought, I realized SHE validated me and all that I believed in: That is a teachers' reward. Teachers set the standards, hopefully very high, not evident in the "finest" schools in our county. They learn it through their acquired focus - finely tuned and honed during their developing years.

The "snap judgments" made by a majority of students and graduates today have been beset by negative emotions. Learned. I used the following lesson for students who by and large couldn't get over their "baggage" and allow their issues to become an overwhelming situation. Rather than seeking out "blame", I used a simple, effective lesson:

A. Start with a clear glass of water : "This is you, in all your purity and posit of self-awareness". INNOCENT.
B. Apply a story to use the following food coloring: Something/Anything (" girl/boy friend stood you up for another date: you found out: she/he complete denial, claiming its not 'your business'). Add: colors appropriated how you feel....

1. Yellow for fear ...add
2. Blue for sadness... murky green...add

3. Green for jealousy ...worse...and
4. Red for anger and the distortion of colors becomes obvious!

And each time a color is added, the water turns that much more murky, and indefinable.

C. To rid themselves of these harsh emotions, I would assure them there is a way to learn to be your own person (use the "Magic words..... of Healing") ......

"I forgive you" as you slowly mix or stir in Bleach.' Notice you're not the same person as you began! This is because of the learning process and your ability that many people don't have; an ability to forgive, REGARDLESS". Stories of life....stories that create baggage and deter our path. The Golden color (left by the bleach) confirms the lesson. Forgiveness... a beautiful thing! Gets one out of the labyrinth that life throws at all of us - forces us to choose a path, hopefully a forgiving one. To rise above the pettiness and become self-aware.

A simple PS: Be sure to dump all of the used materials so students do not take that Golden hue as a solution to their: "baggage". Bleach is poison!

The value we place on learning has pristinely folded itself into nice, technological packages. Carefully sealed and jealously guarded throughout one's lifetime or expense account, they are continuously updated. It's a 'valueless' society with a future spent on the grasshopper's lament: "Oh, the world owes me a living". The New American Dream.....and A New Lost Generation. What future can be saved for them? Can someone say Pension plan? Hahahahahahahahahah! Aggh!

The cell phone has taken away face-to-face conversations and replaced it with nonsensical banter that no one would dare say in public. Texting takes away empathy and intimacy as well! And this is our popular choice du jour. Our Choice. The more we can replace our wallets and pocket purses; rather than exercise an ability to be creative and communicate; with a beep from a carrying phone, we become less "human". Respond? HOW? Where is the owning of one's self? The AUTHENTICITY?

The printed word may soon be next....How few students cannot write 'script'...a dying practice replaced by the timely, time-untested No Child Left Behind Act where someone, or ones, of greater political influence, re-invents the wheel: Replacing it with the computer/laptop. Now other "less important matters" can be replaced: Lets get rid of Art, Dance, Foreign Languages, extra- curricular activities: cheer leading, lacrosse, soccer, school dances, school newspaper: save the taxpayer dollars? Socialization? We don't need no stinkin' socialization.......we got the new Mega multi-faceted 12 point digital color contrast to touch cellular phone/pad! Dick Tracy would be proud. Who do we forgive, and again, HOW?

I would go down the school hallways uttering, maybe a slight bellowing : "Baaaa, Baaaa" as if teachers understood what the students didn't.

And the sheep follow....They never separate from the herd...

A Plan for Starting [New] Teachers /Recognizing Stress

"People always want to give you free advice: that was something I always tried. But you get what you pay for - that's what I say. Now I'm paying and paying and paying. "(Morphine-"Starting Over From Scratch").

Teacher enters the class and writes his/her name on the board for the first day of college student/interns seeking to teach Social Studies: "Good Morning, class".

Invariably, the class is silent, not knowing what to think; No Reply.

With the grumble-mumbling that students who are possibly 'opinionated' or afraid of being first to respond, the teacher, without any emotion to said murmuring, turns back outside to leave the class. Another pause - for the class to evaluate between each other, and, this aloof teacher.

Teacher re-enters, "Good morning class" without changing the intonation from the previous opening of class.

"Good morning, Mr Beauregardi"......most responsive. "Just like most students, you also seek not to have Homework on the first day of class. It has become a learned curse word. Not cool!

It is more than possible that you did not greet me because you did not know my name or, talking with your professor may have been something you have most likely learned from an earlier experience as not prudent.

Yet, you do not know this teacher nor this class - a class as told/given to you by your counselor...So, let's call this our first learning moment: that is, common courtesy should not have to be taught in the classroom. I am not here for that reason...I am your teacher: you may hate me, like me, WHATEVER me, but I do promise you shall receive, from me, the best possible education this curriculum and teacher has to offer- in ALL facets of the outside global community: all that I possibly can.

If you feel threatened - intimidated by this teacher and my 'ways', I would strongly suggest that you seek out your Guidance Counselor as soon as it becomes possible, so as NOT to waste your, my, and those who wish an education: all of our time and efforts. They should not be slighted."

Heads will turn, even a few more mumbles. No short interlude....follow to "Take out a sheet of paper and do NOT, I repeat: DO NOT put your name on it".

The quizzical look is now turning into bewilderment.

"On the top line of the paper, define: 'What is a teacher?' Hold off filling this in right now:

On the other side of the paper, Answer the question: 'What situation/s would make you give up upon the field of Education/ teacher as a profession'.

Take another sheet, (again fill out nothing yet): Explain: Do you feel that schools fail neighborhoods or neighborhoods fail schools- please site from your own experiences: 'EXAMPLES'.

On the other side of this second paper (keeping up with me): What would happen if tenure never existed for teachers?

(pause)

Remember: this is Anonymous, so try to be honest and use all your previous knowledge or even life experiences to answer these."

When the class finishes this, the teacher collects and then has them shuffled, reading another view of their answered questions - one question at a time seeking feedback directed by the teacher is a good learning experience of other,s points of view on sensitive educational topics. The door opens……

Aside from the expected feedback: agree/disagree and the "What if…" scenarios offered in their own papers, the teacher should chime in.

"Notice that we are all different: with different experiences and life changing events that shape or mold our ways of thinking, or even 'being'. Thank Goodness we are not Stepford people: what a boor that would be! This is why so many of you have so many different reasons for becoming a teacher- Is there a right or a wrong in any of this? I contend that if you were honest with your answers, the Anonymous paper cannot place you in any jeopardy regarding your grade in this class: Yes I know you worry about that; what should all this tell you? (there will be incidents where some students reading the others' papers will blurt out "I said that " with their own explanations]. A learning environment has been established.

"Can you see how the Anonymous clause established in the beginning of this lesson creates a self-exposure to give an honest appraisal to pertinent educational questions? The Anonymous clause works very well with high school students too because they have been geared into the "caught up" with numbers-grades and fear an answer that the teacher would not respect would reflect upon them in a negative evaluation. It is known as buying the lie. As a High School Social Studies teacher, I would do this two times with my students, in the scheduled school year: first time, before Christmas (and the middle of the second MP). the second time, before Final exams. The students would need an academic relief from the pressures felt from all classes and their finals. Maybe for my own edification….This was done in "The Best of Times"………

I feel this validates a teacher's growth within a class - even though the numbers should not be the best indicator of what a teacher, or student has acquired or learned in said class.

The classes are teaching the new teacher: note that many teachers would never even come close to allow students an honest appraisal of the class: I can honestly say my students' GPA improved as the they became aware of the class curricula and the teacher's differentiating methodology, as well as one-to one handling of the disaffected, or a student 'baggage'. This is a learning experience for the teacher, sometimes comes early, sometimes later.

"How are you seen by your students: does this matter?" The teacher asks the orientating students: the baggage students or the disaffected ones: can make your lessons change? How drastically will be up to you; how much credence do you give to these individuals. This, this is one of the greatest challenges facing a new teacher: not only with the classroom but with all other facets of their lives! Baggage? You want to know baggage? Let me tell you of….("Here we go AGAIN" something many students heard from their parents as well as the disgruntled, overworked, underpaid experienced beyond self-control teacher). The under paid, overworked teacher would concede: "Maybe if I just control them……."

A teaching experience or moment? Possibly… But it needs to be handled in the 'third person'. Never "I". The Board of Education will claim this not to exist in the curriculum and does not constitute for your preaching to the choir. But,:

Past experiences
Psychological Defenses
Physiological reactions
Coping
Illness behaviors

These series of stressful life events will become the greatest 'killer' of teachers. Students have their baggage too. But their responses are different. Adults contend with them as well: so we are also 'inferring' without mentioning, the supporters of these children. All God's children got stress, and who never experienced unintended consequences?

Stressful Life Events for Educators; can be observed from the Psychological Studies of Holmes-Rahe Social Readjustment Rating Scale (SRRS). Conducted cross-culturally regarding "Life Changing Units" that could apply to events in the past year of an individual's life: this has been done with subsequent validation. The internet can be useful, when the source is understood.

These tests have different SRRS between students and their baggage and teaches with theirs. Yet adults with stress have some risks that students do: Stress,,,,,,it needs to be addressed: i can guarantee teachers feel varied forms of stress daily...whether they are willing to share it or not.

Why do I harp so much upon that which seems so obvious and non-significant to the class?

These stressors happen to everyone and they may already be a part of your life at this very moment: to deal with them and the new job: Teaching itself as a major Stressor (I believe) can affect your output or effectiveness as a qualified teacher.

So.... what are these great stresses that make us who we are in our decision makings/choices in life? I site a source from the internet (from R&M Seminars); Students baggage may not appear as all similar to the stessors as compared with adults: but closer inspection shows they are just as 'human' as the rest of us 'more experienced stressed' (Holmes-Rahe Stress Scale: Adolescence/Wikipedia). And "There lies the rub"....for so many students with little to no life experiences that, at their age, may NOT be willing to approach their own caregiver/parent to seek out advice regarding Stressors such as Dating, Sex, loss of a parents job, or even loss of a parent.

For teachers I find the best answer for any question that may arise from doubting one's self, or their reaction to stress, is SLEEP! If something dwells upon the teacher….. And a loss of sleep results, this individual needs to address that situation the next day…but carefully! Lawsuits abound when a teacher expects a student to confide in them something that they possibly shared with someone who has no idea how to deal with said problem, or maybe even someone they respect that cannot deal with the matter on such a personal level. Guidance or Social Services should be addressed, after the student is told of this action by the teacher- no surprises for anyone: "I have to let you know that I cannot give you any personal advice, in that, fearing I could be wrong or, the advice may be completely out of the context of your life-stress situation, I am going to send you to the Guidance Office so that they may get a better handle on your situation: I am sorry if this may offend your opinion of me or how you may reflect upon this class, but this is part of my contract and I am afraid for you." An unwanted pregnancy would be a perfect example. If you can't sleep, something is wrong.

For students its different, as they are individuals: they may feel their parents don't understand, so they may confide in friends, cousins, or may just keep the door closed and try to ignore it, or, to alleviate the immediacy of hurt they feel individually, turn to a drug or the drug culture; accepting it as a "one time event ". It may be one time, but coping with that event can be threatening or challenging for an adolescent. A wrong turn in the Labyrinth of life can be life - altering: the Stressors students will most likely have to face in one form or another, creates the idea of the individual and choice. "Choice is Freedom" is one of my more favorite cliches, and they need to know that feeling they are without a choice, someone or something else will be determining how their life will be. But choosing wisely can often answer a cry for help: an option is another choice.

"Jerry Maguire" said it best: "Help me to help you"…. Prevention cannot always be the first [and probably most effective] solution; but as mentioned above there are a great many support services that will at least give a better direction to whatever the problem(s) student or students may be experiencing.. Oh yes, you can now get to sleep.

Wake up!

What if said student does not show for class that next day…. or, cuts the class or even shows up in a mood that gives every indication that the wrong was not 'righted'. Once shame on you, twice, shame on me: this is the time for action for the teacher. …. … . . Not to be calling home, though; that could signal a continuation or further abuse that the student does not need. Time for the teacher to meet with the Guidance Counselor or Social Services and air concerns. You may not be the significant other that the student or parents want. This is not the role of a concerned teacher: as much empathy that you may show or try, the old adage, "Give an inch and they'll take a mile" can also become "let sleeping dogs lie"! If you want to exact a positive/preventive approach, let the aforementioned people do their job: these problems should not allow you to play the "middle man". This is their job: they do it quite well. In the concern of 'everything' you had experienced with this individual previously, in and out of class, a teacher can always follow up: to make sure that there is a plan of action and an understanding between said individual and the Counselor/Services.

So it is not too hard to believe that they are swamped with varied stressors involving their students as well as performing their job to a livable level for all concerned: to meet the challenges the next day….and every next day thereafter. Empathy is a good thing, giving too much is not. The teacher needs to find that balance: I always felt that announcing (as early as possible) that this teacher will be "firm but fair".

This is where the Anonymous scoring of the teacher applies: after they get more than just a whiff of what is expected of them in your class. And so you read over the 5 anonymous questions (see above) and discover that you are not everyone' hero. Oh, the shame of it all: did you lose any students with your challenges, or did they respond: even a negative response can be a learned one. REMEMBER; YOU CAN'T SAVE EVERYONE. A new teacher can sit in on other classes and see for themselves those teachers who refuse to use any form of discipline find that there is a lack of control issues abound ("I want to be your friend") and, even though they may give respect, this does not guarantee their getting respect. Students know which teacher they can get away with certain aspects of learning or even caring. Button pushers from the early days of primary school, you can care, but you cannot expect the same in return as a reflex action. Hopefully learned by example.......

Firm but fair.

Student can act out in a negative ways toward another - an obvious bullying tactic. A very simple outburst towards a class disruption, the teacher needs to say nothing but to simply walk over to the computer (and all students fear for their grade, still expecting firm but fair). the teacher, without a word to either student (who may be preparing a blame -game), hit the space bar three to four times. PARANOIA!

"What....What did you do......you change my grade? I didn't do anything-he started it with his talking about my mother! That's not fair".... A very quick retort "We'll talk about it later, after class"....and with that done, break exactly back to where the class had been before the disruption: no dwelling. If the student cares enough, they will stay after. All can be revealed, with the promise: "Once shame on you. Next time I will miss the space bar"....Surprisingly, most students already realize what their grade is, so no arguing should ensue. If the teacher feels the other student was bullying, the same applies here. Judgment call is a learned behavior.

One thing a decent teacher should remember in these one-to-one conversations/revelations: If the student 'exaggerates' or has a propensity to make a whale out of a minnow, remember the not to 'assume', old adage. It may be some other baggage:

so follow -up the talk with "Who do you feel safe with? Are you talking to your Mom? Do you feel safe with her?" If the answer is 'Yes' to these questions, the next statement should be obvious: "Mama la sabe toda" or, Mother knows best. "Maybe you should speak to her before I or anyone else says anything to her: Don't you think she would rather hear this 'incident' from you before the school gives its version?" That may just put the kibosh on the baggage that may not be as heavy as one you may have thought. Nevertheless: if a student even mentions they are not safe, or bear the marks, grades, physical, or emotional, the teacher still needs to take some affirmative action.

THE ANOSOGNOSTIC COCALORUM

Anosognosis: Not knowing of a condition one suffers: unaware of one's own disability.

Baggage?

Often used in medical terms; yet since 'anon' means 'without' and 'gnossis' meaning 'knowledge', a more modern definition has been applied: "Too stupid to know you are stupid". Ask any Psychologist.

I would be remiss if I did not relate 2 incidents here that applied to Holmes and Rahe Stress Inventory that likely could happen to any teacher. It appears to me that this 'deficit of self-awareness', would be evident in anyone who may exhibit a 'Napoleonic', Type A personality, or ie: compensation with a superiority personality [AlzOnline.net: Anosognosis, 2007]. Nevertheless........

What a mouthful....

App. 2008 and a new Administrator had been added to the HS. An outsider from a very prominent school and known from the wrestling/golf team as "Chillio", developed a rapport that was admired through the district. Affluent... and showing great humility towards others, he was easily the top of his class. I thought it to be a good Idea to take it upon myself and congratulate him on this sudden promotion from Physical Ed teacher to an Assistant Principal.

"I just wanted to come by and say congrats to Chillio" with my hand out.

That's where it stayed: Out …..And empty.

"First of all, my name is Mr K…and I will not tolerate being called by any other name". I am cooked for the year…sticks a fork in me. He would continue in a verbal lambasting of me as if he was Truman and I was Hiroshima. This Draconian manner I sat through, due to the fact that I would not be baited by such a newbie/tyrant. In retrospect, he must have been protecting himself in his space…Mother Teresa said: *It's not about them and you, it's about you and God"*.

His scathing monologue was drowned out by Shakespeare in my head: "More to pity than to blame." The best I could surmise was that he must have feared the position he was in and when a puppet's strings get pulled correctly, they will do anything you want. Mine were not….I summoned up the intestinal fortitude that I had, stood upon his ending rant with a sought after retort: "I still wanted to say congratulations on your promotion." He said nothing. I turned and walked out. I feel that, as a senior member of the faculty, it was his intention to have me go off on a wild tangent to other teachers on the rumor mill, of what this new Administrator's Mission Statement was….I knew and would not feed his "flash fire'. Absolute Power corrupts absolutely.

This is going to be an interesting year.

One time in particular, the class President for seniors, Lyan P, ran into the back of my room while I was in mid-lecture. "Mr. B! You gotta help me, Mr. K is in the hall and is looking to nail me…I was in the cafeteria"…..knowing this task master and his opportunity to make THE strict example he so wanted, I hid the student under my desk where a teacher sets his/her legs.

As abruptly as Lyan entered, so did the new VP…said nothing to no one: stood and paced the back of the room looking down each aisle. I had stopped, then, without acknowledgment, continued my lecture. After a few minutes of Inspector Clouseau, he had left. I told Lyan to remain in the class for a security reason {safety, really] and I told the class to trust their teacher and remain quiet of this. Lagrand students know this lesson well, they've lived it. After 10 minutes, I had a student check the hallway, on way to the bathroom: the hallway was clear and Lyan went on his way. I know I gained a friend or two this day: Thanks, Chillio.

Neat thing about Lyan was that he could trust me because his mother was a student in my first year of teaching. Experience has its own rewards...This one was sweet. The meeting at Graduation? Priceless!

To say my year would be momentous would be a joke! On a cold winter day where I was given the "Duty" as all teachers are assigned one, the hallway was freezing and I was expected to sign students in right at the outside door/hall entrance. Cold regardless. Chillio's revenge! The sign -ins were always many for this VP because he would make the cutting class an intolerable act. OK...hope it works... But his domain was his office, no one dared to enter the lair. No one showed for 10 minutes before the next class, so I handed in the sign-ins to Mr. K....As he was admonishing me for not being an "even good teacher"; he knew I would not respond to his blistering...BUT, as I left through the drama stage backroom for class, I quietly said " Cocalorum"... and continued my pace...

"What did you just say, Mr Beauregardi?" His voice rose to the heights of his pitch. "Nothing, just complaining about the floorboards between this door and the hall'. Yeah, you're going to intimidate me.....

Just in case you asked:

COCALORUM: A self-important little man

The other incident involved a student from my class who wished to come in while I was teaching the next class. He knew, as I knew, this was a ploy to make a nuisance of himself, outside of the class. I walked over to the door, and told the student to

"Go away". .He insisted to continue, and I continued to make my point in lecture. I then went back to the door and, opening my door, asked him what part of the two-letter word did he not understand. "no is NO".

"You can,,,,,,,,,MY.....!"

"Excuse me?" I said, knowing exactly what he said..... Validation! ; "What was that? Did you say.....my......?" By this time I had a number of his friends surround me at my door egging me to do something....Teachers around me in adjacent rooms avoided the incident: even closing their doors as their voices rose to a crescendo. Hallway guard Bell was doing his best to get down the hallway.

"Did you hear this student? He told me to....his....." I repeated so that there was no controversial give-and-take regarding what was said to precipitate this. This student's compatriots started to prance around me like a whirling dervishes and made a thumb and forefinger gun up to my head to antagonize me to react physically.

The said student was finally taken away by Bell, as I watched my neighboring teachers stare out their doors. The student claims he was trying to get his cell phone back from another in my class. All a farce...and, all my fault.

I received no support from any teachers and was told the said culprit was given 2 days out-of-school suspension, to which he returned to school the next day to "get His books". Familiar pattern: Hanging out with his friends-waiting for me, in the hallway, to respond....I knew the cameras around me were operating, so I stood there...Oblivious....... and kept returning to my room to call and get some assistance. I expected too much.

The threat to withhold my increment for the following year [a new administrator, not surprising] was one of two punishments that I received for my repeating the students' abusive words: Firstly, I had been given the memo that I was no longer to be the AP World History teacher: that I would only need to prepare one prep. A kiss of Death: I expressed my disdain for this, something many teachers probably would have relished: but not me. I had developed this class from its inception: wrote the curriculum through the summer to make it compatible with the standards placed on the AP Co-coordinators demands for college accreditation. "This is like taking away my Baby!"...I stated; "I created this..... I am the only one who knows this material. You are doing the students and me a great disservice." The other teachers said to me that this was being done for me and would make my day easier. I was supposed to be thankful.

The next day there was a message written on the back board of my room: "Hey, Mr Beau, D...is going to get you, man." So the gang outside my class that day were more of a vigilante/ posse. Threatening me, I told my Administrator, who promptly came down and just stared at the written comment directed at me. I made sure that the VP saw me take pictures of this quote... She continued to stand and stare at it. With nothing said, I felt I was being asked to respond to this affront. "Maybe I should call the police, because this threat is a considered assault", but still no response except: "I will take care of this". So am I to think I should be living in fear for the rest of my years in Lagrand? I was assured that it all would be taken care of..... nice and sooo assuring. I started to begin walking down the hallway and making the sound: "pffft....pffft," with a motion to pull the arrows out of my back...this union's not out to help the individual, only teachers who seek out new contracts in bulk and bundle. Pay raise and Medical! Forgiveness is Golden.

But, Stress......can come from everywhere. OK, so I have become a target.

I rise above the fray during the Holiday season: red footprints on the ceiling and the board for Halloween; and my special moment. Lunch time the pumpkin bought gets cut, with the cooking room allowing me [they trust me] to bake the seasoned pumpkin seeds.

Just like union meetings, the teachers would wander/gather for a taste of Thanksgiving, ala Beau (Unions: If you bring food, they will come). I motivated my students during class to offer a way for giving back to their own, ones they knew but would not publicly mention: Santa's Diaper Brigade. A gift of giving.

The Brigade was started to prevent the cycle of "kids having kids, having kids". To buy diapers for the needy students who are STILL attending school, yet have a mother or grandmother watching their baby, I initiated an M&M sale. Photo pics of me in China, varied Christmas ornaments and phrases were put on sale: green-white-red colors: fifty cents for three from a candy dispenser. Some kids kept my M&Ms as a keepsake in their locker until the last day of school! Students were told I would match the amount that was collected for this cause. The local supermarket has an Answer! 15 packs of diapers were sent to the Guidance Office for them to determine who was most needy in accepting this Santa/gift.

Some of the posse, though, relished the idea of having a "trophy" from a misled, taken-advantage-of 15 year old teen [yes some even 14]. They would strut with their "trophy" and impregnated girlfriends who would follow them everywhere. The heartbreak at home and the readjustments forced to make on the parents and teen child must have been a tremendous stressor. Someone has to care: and doing the right thing can at least draw some positive attention to [maybe] the PTA, or the Board of Education, or maybe even the Administration. Though the cream always comes to the top, most educators have a cynical view one could call sour cream.

I cherished and reveled to have seen each student, who found time in their busy day, with our Guidance choice and approval, to thank me for their diapers over the Holidays. Blessings.....

I believe it was Sir Edmund Burke, speaking out in England's Parliament to emphasize his view of the American Revolutionary War:

> *"All that evil needs to flourish and thrive is for good men to do nothing."*

Reward? Are you kidding?..I got it ten-fold from the teen mothers. I also made sure to let them know, they are not forgotten......Merry Christmas.

SAMPLES

There has been one Professional Development teacher that made the greatest impact upon my capabilities to teach. He came in the beginning of the year early in my teaching career. He was Dr Harry Wong and his message was one of simplicity: "Steal Everything"! Whoa...The seventh commandment...But, if a teacher needs at a moment notice: paper/a marker/an eraser/a textbook [or two]/a pencil/pen/sharpener? As one plans out their lesson strategies, spending time with the filing and seating charts and who cut and paperwork for lesson plans, validate them. Needless time gets spent. True I did not sit in on other classes, but this was a "necessary and proper" clause.

If a lesson I used worked well and needed a little tweaking to make it as fair as possible while still motivation and inspiring students, I used the following two lessons for all Chapters of History: World and/or US that would create a better understanding of the chapter vocabulary

1. Puzzlemaker.com

A teacher may apply one of several choices to use for the vocabulary and geographic usage. Crosswords did challenge the students' abilities to answer a statement. They can also be rearranged so that same answer would be in a different part of another puzzle.

"What did you get for 4 across?"

"RhineRiver": remember no spaces are counted on a crossword.

"That can't be: Jesus did not cross the Rhine River." So borrowing answers becomes a chore for those who rely on others. This still makes for a great review of the Chapter: note to remember it is a crossword puzzle, so, suggest a pencil! When they take their test, they will realize the Crossword was really a vocabulary check!

2. Jeopardy

Teacher selects the 5 most important categories that are consistent in the chapter. Then, listing in order of difficulty, write them on an index card in increments of ten (10/20/30/40/50). On the board will be a grid of the five selected categories in chart form, similar to the TV show. The teams are not in groups but in rows, so that no one can dominate the board. The nest correct question is answered for the following student who got the earlier "question'. ANSWERS MUST BE IN THE FORM OF A QUESTION. This allows all students to pay attention to a slip-up of a right answer not in the form of a question. Its the next hand raised outside the team row that gets the opportunity to question the answer.

Let's try Spelling for 10… Students immediately feel this is the cake category: until they get "Mesopotamia" for 10 points (What is…). All answers increase with difficulty and no one is allowed to jump ahead of their favorite part of the Chapter. This way the board stays controlled, avoiding domination. Minus points are assigned Homework! This is to be avoided at all costs by the row, since the Jeopardy game is known to be in reverse the next day as a TEST.

Only during the Final Jeopardy answer are the rows to be allowed to discuss their question that I will not give until each row sees what the other rows have tallied… the reward for winning Jeopardy is 10% added to their test grade!

"Your final Jeopardy answer will be in the category of Geography"…Now the students are shifted from rows to a collaborative group to determine who knows Geography and how well. One thing that slips by many of the students is the phrase of Alec Trebek: "Remember to put your response in the form of a Question". Students should realize that whatever they wager should only be seen by the teacher, and not heard by any other team member. So, BEFORE THE FINAL JEOPARDY ANSWER is given out, the teacher must check each row to see what they wish to wager on this last Answer. This ensures no abrupt changing of the wager once they hear my final answer: a 7 to a 1. a 3 to an 8.

Once the test is given on the next day...what they got wrong on Jeopardy, they get right on the test. Reversal: Answer-to-question and question-to answer. They recognize this and request more Jeopardy because of its value to prepare students to know what they don't know.

PS: How many students do you think got the answer right for the Final Jeopardy, while forgetting to put it in the form of a question????? RIOT!!!!!!!!!!!! Over learning?

PIN-OCCHIO

By this time one can make a conclusion that all Education is not sun and roses. When the moment arises that a team sport loses, a student has a fight in the lunchroom, a problem at home, etc., I have found a winning technique to create a hero from a goat. Of interest, I would have this little "ego booster" done in every class, at least once: This to validate the student who is rarely recognized by the class population: and should be. Invariably, the following has always happened....and it works!

"If this class cannot be quiet, it appears that the remainder of this lesson will need to be done at home...in other words [here it comes] ...HOMEWORK!

Ah, man, and the permeating mumble-grumble of the students, in particular, those who were paying attention. "Hey Mr. B...That's not fair to give homework to all of us! Why not just assign it to the ones making the noise", "An interesting proposition: and your teacher does want to be fair....and all of you are not acting out.

So, here's what is going to happen (their attention is 100%):

I have in my hand a staple: See?" This is part of the plot that needs to be addressed, being it is so small. "When I drop this staple, I should be able to hear it…meaning the class is quiet enough to forego the before-assigned homework. Now, if I don't hear it, then the class needn't seek an easy assignment: FOR ALL!

Two things here: first, it is a wonder to watch the students police themselves as the teacher holds the staple high in the air. "Shut up man, I got a game today and I don't want any homework" and " Why don't you just shut up" then, "No, why don't you!" and an argument may ensue….Easily solved with the teacher announcing "Here we go!" And start a 3-2-1 countdown….

Also of note: dropping a staple on almost any floor makes no sound, at least for the human ear to pick up….

Enter a student from the Bathroom: "Hey, man,: I was…"

"Shut up, man; we're gonna get homework if Mr. B doesn't hear that staple"….The entering student will expect an explanation…But there's no time for it…"3.."

"Just shut up!" The class yells in unison….

"OK, I'll start again: "3…..2 "and then the snickering would kick in…."Hey, if I get homework because of YOU, we're going to have some words outside the class later!"…

Oh, the AAAAgony…AAAgony of it all: inside I am laughing, then realize that this isn't being very fair to those concerned students.

Not the motivation sought. So as I bring my hand down to wait for the quiet, I do the devious deed: I SWITCH the staple to my other hand…..And then hold my first hand up again, to the Count Down (with no staple, this time).

"3…2……1: and I separate my fingers as if I dropped the staple: Ah there's the rub!

It's easy to guess the response of the class: "I heard it-I heard it-Me, too" at least 7-8 of them….Teacher is expressionless: for they begin to realize that its the teacher who needs to determine sound vs Homework. "I didn't hear it" I say calmly. At this point I look through the class, looking for that wallflower of a student: one who is quiet to the extreme and would rather have their arm ripped off than to raise it for a question or an answer.

"Maybe I am right and the quiet was not enough…but maybe I am wrong… Me? Wrong? I suppose that is possible. So, let's be fair….Juana…" Her head shoots up as quickly as the class' heads turn toward her. "You'd better say you heard it!" One of the 'I heard it's' blurts out. As a teacher, I know my choice is correct.

I sit next to Juana-saying in a calm voice"Forget him: forget that anyone is here…just think and react to my reason why you think that I may have chosen you beyond anyone else…. Look at me: I trust you, trust and believe you, right?" "Yes" the response. "I know what peer pressure is and I am sure you do, too: I know you realize what that effect has on anyone subjected to it. So, now I ask you: Can you honestly say you heard the staple?"

"No".

The groans are Charlie Brown-esque…"AAAAGH"…..

"She was right: For here is the same staple in my other hand". As I raise the staple in my left hand, the roar of approval has a matching affect upon the student and the teacher: I suppose the rest of the class at some level. Maybe they realized their Pinocchio-nose was growing! "Look to see if there is a staple on the floor."

"The class has no homework"…" YEEESSS," and the beam that shined of Juana remains: "Juana has set a standard for the class that hopefully can follow you for the rest of your life…. And the few of you who heard something where something was nothing to hear?…Well, the nurse is on the way to the cafeteria, so we'll forget that, since I know you hear me now, Right?" Who would be the sheep in THIS class? The whole idea of fact vs truth has been proved: If you believe, that is your truth…yours and yours alone."

Juana has set aside the peer pressure and can now think for herself: The class has visibly watched the rock pushed and accomplished.

At the end of class: "Thanks, Juana" they says on their way out…and Juana?

She has found a part of herself that was always there.

"And always let your conscience be your guide". (Jiminy Crickett)

MICHELANGELO

OK: As promised I have something prepared for you that I feel will not only reflect the rebirth of Knowledge, or the Renaissance, but will give you a clear indication of what life was like for the people of that era.

The Sistine is considered one of the greatest masterpieces of Christian Art. Michelangelo was a sculpture, who understood the cutting/honing /chipping and polishing a figure that was to emerge as the individual hidden in that rock. "May God save my soul" was his response when he was asked to paint the Chapel by the Pope. Today, the holiest day for the Christian world, Easter, mass is said under the work of Michelangelo: like much of History, many painters had attempted to add or delete much of Michelangelo's work, yet the modern day Restoration process: painstakingly renewed by the Church, has revealed some very human qualities over the candle-soot and salt cracks that time and re- painters had "filmed over'. Results are "stunning" by most who have seen this holy work of art.

From Christus Rex.com, I have taped for each student a copy of the centerpiece of the Sistine Chapel, aptly known as "The Creation'. This painting is believed to depict God touching Adam to give him Life. Maybe though, since this is the humanism movement where all figures holy or otherwise, are given a 'human' quality. I offer you this question: Is it God giving Life to Adam, or could it be Adam granting that God is real to answer all the unanswered questions of man's existence, thus creating God? Remember, this is the Renaissance Era and much of what existed was known to have been "God's will". What do you think?

Back to the taped paper that you have realized by now Jhangs from the edge of your desk down for you to refer to underneath the desk. Using the tape I have supplied for you (a good teacher is like a good scout), use this blank sheet of paper I am handing out for you to tape UNDERNEATH your desk.... That way you will be recreating the efforts of Michelangelo as he painted the centerpiece of the Sistine: ON HIS BACK.

"I am bent like a Syrian Bow" he is known to have said... Music of the time period will create the moment that was one time Michelangelo's. AHH, but most teachers know the next words out of their class's mouths:

"My back hurts"

"My arm hurts"

"This is too awkward"

The teacher has made a point already: Now you find yourself guilty of the modern day, highly shortened work ethic. You are witnessing one individual's diligence/dedication/devotion to one's faith...In those days there was little else: work from sun up to sun down, 6 days a week, and Sunday Mass. And since the mass was said in Latin and not the vernacular (of the people), what did people have to educate themselves to understand the Holy scriptures? Forget school... Work for food led to larger families: Latin was only for the noblesse oblige.

Paintings (pictures)! With "human" qualities that the masses could relate to.

Those students complaining of their arms/backs hurting them should know that they have been complaining in an amazing 4 minutes time: Michelangelo spent four YEARS working on the Sistine Chapel ceiling. The power of faith that he had, we should only venture to wish we had ourselves. Michelangelo's persistence is a virtue!

So, don't short-change yourself...your efforts define you: not the numeric grade, not the kid who sit next to you in the cafeteria, and certainly not your peers.

DANTE'S INFERNO

With curiosity piqued after this lesson, the most obvious follow-up would be the antithesis: Hell. Background information is always helpful, to enlighten the new Renaissance learners, even those who are excuses bound why they not had read the assignment.

With the invention of Gutenberg's Printing Press, books became more accessible as well as affordable. Unfortunately, the Nobility of the day had the wealth; their desire was to have books done in their Papal language, Latin. But Dante was not of the nobles' beliefs: he felt that a great injustice had been done to the peasantry by having the book that all were expected to understand, The Bible, in the nobles' language. Since most printing shops were set up around Churches, the priests were now making money by having not only the Bible in 'print', but the selling of the forgiveness of sins, known as 'indulgences'. These "licenses" to sin could only be afforded by, who else, the nobles! Can you imagine the deals made by the Church: "two sins for the price of one!" And the peasants...... just needed to forego sin....

Enter Dante with his idea to have his Divine Comedy printed in the language of the people! If cheap enough, which it was, the peasants could read of all the sins of the nobility and Church. Done in the vernacular, or Italian, this forced the hand of the nobilities to do a reverse and learn the language of the people. Italian for the Italian people. Therefore the Printing Press shook the foundations of the Church control and created a new opportunity for the working class to learn to Read (Martin Luther was very aware of this)!

Nobility? They tried to burn the books, but they were printed that much faster: who, therefor, didn't want to know if they had been labeled for one of Dante's 9 levels of Hell? For the class, the funnel shape levels of Dante's Inferno would be placed on the board. They laugh at the city of Dis, since it has become a common phrase of the hallway: "Who you be Dissin"? I like to propose to these students that they may know something of this, but were they aware of this city in the middle of Dante's Inferno when they "be Dissin"?

One level would be pointed out: with the word "Usurers". Bankers to us. Today there may be a few people that believe bankers are residents of Hell. Sinful? Really? What if you can't afford a car/house/education/ and the list can go on.

Since the morals of our society have changed with time, if it were YOUR decision to create a new, more modern version of Hell, what would you keep, and what would you get rid of? The greatest sin? The least of sins....The class gets motivated when they are given the assignment to place modern day people they have heard/learned of in their own Hell. As Dante did, they could also appoint a "Divine Retribution" performed upon their occupants of their Hell.

One need only read "People" magazine to determine their infamous sinners. There are some students, though, that refer back to World History to list the greatest evil humans that they know. A word of caution: when it gets personal: seek the Guidance Counselor...Toot Suit!

"Thus Conscience Makes Cowards of Us All"
(Hamlet:Shakespeare)

Jiminy C would probably argue this quote, and, as that I am now retired, I suppose I am somewhere in between them. The past and the future...The "Never gonna Be's" and the 'Wanna Be's". The reasoning to write this? Strike while the iron is hot...and my memory has yet to have been fully overcome by a selective Alzheimer's. I wanted carpe diem...to seize the day: Everyday as I was a teacher and still sharing. Like a beggar playing music: casting pearls before swine and refusing to allow the gullible to be easily preyed upon by the innocent.

A few times in class I allowed a use of "conscience" to literally "Wake Up" a student whose baggage had him down and out for the count (asleep).

"Lou" I whispered in the ear of the proposed sleeping student.

"Lou, this is your conscience speaking to you, Lou…..I am sure you hear me, Lou…What will your parents say to you if your teacher calls them to say you are not getting enough sleep at night? Sleeping in class, Lou? Do you have an answer that is true for your conscience? Why not wake up, Lou and be the person your parents love and would be proud of": Then the teacher slowly rises from whispering to the teenage Somnambulist… and nudges the leg of said student's chair. They always wake up; most with a yawn, to which I chuckle, inside.

Then I continue to lecture without missing a step….or comment.

I push the rock

Same as it ever was. I love teaching.

Karli K. February 14, 2008

My Most Important Lesson Learned

Throughout the past ten years of my education I would strive year after year to earn my grades. I always expected to work to my full potential to prevail over difficult obstacles. Whether it is school or sports, I was always pushed to accomplish my goals. I constantly worried about pleasing everyone. I was always so engrossed to my studies, that I never took a break to think about what I had learned.

After the bus driver arrives and the doors open to my graduation day, I will be free to roam the real world for the rest of my life. Of course, school prepares us for college, but shouldn't it also ready us for the real world? Over the years I had learned different math equations and read a variety of literature, but it wasn't until freshman year that my grades were the most imperative assets I would need to possess for college. Yes, they are exceptionally important, but I also need to be equipped to face the harshest battlefield of all, life.

It was the final marking period of my freshman year and I was hunting for my A in history to make high honor roll. I spoke to my teacher, Mr. Bearegardi, and he gave me numerous extra credit projects to gain the additional points I needed. By the time I was finished with all my work, I had achieved well over an A. As he presented me with my 09 average, I graciously thanked my teacher.

After I had celebrated my small victory, he asked me if I had learned anything. I answered him by saying that I had actually learned. Mr. Beauregardi then explained that a grade was just a number and that it didn't matter if I received an A or F, as long as I had a great experience with history and best of all, that I had learned from it. I used to despise history before I met Mr. Beauregardi.

Everything in life seems to be based on numbers and reaching a certain point. Even being accepted into college is all about numbers and averages. Our futures depend on numbers and being the best, but life doesn't always involve being the best or the richest. Life is about making mistakes and learning to correct them one day at a time. It's about learning lessons and realizing that we can't always be the cream of the crop. We have to learn to accept our faults and not allow them to ruin our goals. This is what I experienced with Mr. Beauregardi. He taught me something I will always cherish. He taught me that it's not always about having the highest average or being the best student, but achieving a new goal and learning something new.

ORIGINAL MESSAGE

Monday, 3 Jun 2013 11:50
Priority: Normal
From Iv R.
Love it! Thank you.
From: Oscar Beauregardi
as per your request::I have far too many favorite/famous quotes, so here are my David Lettermen top 6

6. Failure is the condiment for the flavor of success.
5. Le v ache qui rui
4. Mean Mister Beau sleeps in the park shaves in the dark
3. Gabacci
2. I got a big fat "F" for your refrigerator
1. Such pleasantries should go unnoticed

My most memorable moment: probably very corny by some standards: but it was my being hired to teach at Lagrand, after ten years of subbing and doing menial work. Melancholy because my mother, who always supported and believed in my dedication, did not survive her illness to witness the event.

After retirement will be a pause...................................

Then I will be retracing my father's footsteps through France, since WWII was never a topic he was willing to share with any family member of my family.

I am hoping to understand, POP

FAMILY IN PARIS

I made that opportunity: to follow through with my promise to find and visit the family that my father took care of in WW II. While alive, I tried to get my Pop to come along.....He declined. Made my task even more necessary.

The first people to greet me was the family...Though they did not recognize me, I had an inclination of who they were.

I was treated like a KING...Showed the Eiffel Tower, the Arc de Triumphe, the Lourve, the West Bank, Notre Dame Cathedral, and the tomb of Napoleon. When in Normandy, I had the opportunity of a lifetime to swim where my father landed: Omaha Beach. A severe low tide by my US standards can only mean that this was ideal for a landing by the Allied Forces. Oh, did I mention it was November!

I was amazed mostly at the Palace of Versailles...Immense and culturally something France can be very proud of....The Wax Museum was a marvel: Michael Jackson to Ernest Hemingway to President Obama to Louis XVI....of note: I sat next to a wax figure that slept with a newspaper on a park bench....I sat quietly while two French ladies gazed at him...and then ME! After a half a minute of their arguing, I interjected: "Bonjour!" The screams heard throughout the Museum brought the family over as the 2 ladies took off running for the door!

I was taken told a few of the stories the family told me of Pop and his experiences in Paris:

1. Pop had proposed to Mom before going over...he made his way int occupied territory to help this family in need.
2. The castle that was once held by the Nazis had a moat where Freedom fig were executed. "You can see the bullet marks where the moat was..."
3. Many if the dead Germans lay on the ground, refused to be picked upped f to see. "There's a dead German, there's another...and another" Blase in pointing them out.

ABOUT THE AUTHOR

Oscar. Beauregardi is a retired school teacher with the Masters in Education. The writing of this book was done extremes of consciousness in the processes of learning; of nature and nurture.

He has three children, Maryann, Clint and a new found son, Jay Mitchell. Jay was discovered after a 38 year absence.

His life experiences prompted him to dedicate this book to many people who influence his education. Mostly, Thomas Pery, Thomas Donahue the many different but expressive students and teachers that gave up themselves without prejudice. Mostly my father and mother, Joe and Mary Costa

He has traveled to:

1. Nanjing, China
2. Paris, France
3. The East coast, Sydney, and the outback of Australia
4. Southern California State

www.ingramcontent.com/pod-product-compliance
Lightning Source LLC
Chambersburg PA
CBHW022111050726
47591CB00002B/752